THIS DIARY BELONGS TO

AF284005

....

2024
Astrology Diary

patsy Bennett

ROCKPOOL

A Rockpool book
PO Box 252
Summer Hill
NSW 2130
Australia

rockpoolpublishing.com
Follow us! **f** 🅾 rockpoolpublishing
Tag your images with #rockpoolpublishing

ISBN: 9781922579119
Northern hemisphere edition

Published in 2023, by Rockpool Publishing
Copyright text © Patsy Bennett 2023
Copyright design © Rockpool Publishing 2023

Internal design by Jessica Le, Rockpool Publishing
Cover design and typesetting by Sara Lindberg, Rockpool Publishing
Edited by Lisa Macken

Frontispiece by W.G. Evans, 1856, Map of the Constellations in July, August, September.
Other map illustrations by Alexander Jamieson, 1822, Celestial Atlas.
Glyph illustrations by http://All-Silhouettes.com
Zodiac illustrations by http://vectorian.net
Compass illustration by Jessica Le, Rockpool Publishing

Printed and bound in China
10 9 8 7 6 5 4 3 2 1

NB: the planetary phenomena and aspects listed on each day are set to
Greenwich Mean Time (GMT) apart from the summer time (31 March
to 27 October), where they are set to British Summer Time. To convert
times to your location please see www.timeanddate.com. Astrological
interpretations take into account all aspects and the sign the sun and
planets are in on each day and are not taken out of context.

Introduction

Make this your best year yet! This is the year to think outside the square and to consider how you can innovate, imagine and create a foundation and structure in your life that works for you.

This diary/planner is designed to help you make the most of your year. When you live your life by the sun, moon and stars, you'll love the 2024 Astrology Diary: you'll have expert astrological advice right at your fingertips! I have interpreted major daily astrological data for you here in the diary pages to help you plan ahead so that 2024 will be all you wish it to be.

Simply follow the diary dates, and the interpretations of astrological phenomena will help you to plan ahead and enjoy your days. See 'How to use this diary' for more details about the terminology used in the diary pages.

The major strategies for personal growth and success this year are:

- be prepared to step into new territory
- think laterally
- combine personal goals with humanitarian aims
- be bold
- be practical.

In January, Pluto, the dwarf planet known in astrological terms as the celestial transformer, steps into Aquarius, where it will be for the next 20 years. Pluto in Aquarius will have a generational influence, suggesting people born at this time will be innovators and will wish to change the world. On a personal level, the entry of Pluto into Aquarius in 2024 provides the chance to put projects and new ideas onto a stronger footing, especially those you innovated or set in motion in 2023.

Be prepared to think laterally and consider the best path forward for yourself on a humanitarian, big-picture scale. Effectively, you will be working both on a personal level to create the life you want and on a collective, humanitarian, level – to be productive within the world as it is and to create a world you want.

The moon's north node in Aries will help you take action in areas in which you feel you have a strong sense of purpose, which will create ideal circumstances for you to achieve a sense of fulfilment. The key here is that you must take action: very little will come from simply waiting and hoping that your life will become how you wish it to be.

There will be no planets retrograde from early February until the end of March, making February and March a go-ahead, progressive period as your actions are likely to take effect. This phase will be excellent if you have fantastic plans already underway, but potentially chaotic if you have no plans and nothing in particular you wish to grow or nurture. This is largely because other people's plans will override yours, so be prepared to formulate your plans already in January so you can take advantage of this forward-moving influence.

Luckily, the concurrent and influential sextile (60-degree) aspect between Saturn and Jupiter will be conducive to constructive talks. This sextile will be closest on 5 February, and while this would ordinarily be an ideal date to work towards, bringing fresh ideas and projects into being, it's possible matters will be more complex due to Pluto's entry into Aquarius. This could potentially bring upheaval, so you must be careful to take action in manageable step-by-step stages to avoid difficulties and feeling overwhelmed.

Being practical and patient will be useful skills throughout the year, especially in April, as Mercury will be retrograde from 1 April until 25 April. Communications, travel and projects may not regain steam before mid-May and could slow some of your plans down. It will, nevertheless, be a good time to rethink your plans if you need to.

Luckily, Jupiter, the planet associated with abundance, will be in chatty and business-oriented Gemini, bringing opportunities to network, move around and generally connect mid-year. Jupiter in Gemini will help with negotiations, communications, financial planning and travel from the end of May until early October, so if you're planning major changes in any of these areas then mid-year is your time to act!

June may be a particularly beneficial month in this respect as Saturn, the ruler of money, planning, boundaries and limits, turns retrograde at the end of June, and could slow some projects down afterwards. (If you have a prominent Saturn signature in your natal chart and prefer a slower pace, July and August could still be positive months in which to take action.)

However, if you're looking towards making long-term changes in your life such as relocation or retirement, you are best to set the ball rolling in February or March due to the retrograde Mercury in April. You will gain the opportunity to rethink your plans from May to early October as Pluto, the planet that will bring much of the long-term, transformative change into being both in your personal life and collectively, will be retrograde during that period.

During the third quarter, Saturn and Jupiter will be at a tough angle (a 90-degree angle), and for many this will be a more difficult time to set plans in motion. For some, however, especially air signs Gemini, Libra and Aquarius, the benefit of Mars in Gemini in August will help you push through difficulties to create ideal opportunities for success, especially if you're used to working through adversity.

September and October will be ideal to review and reassess where you are in your progress in 2024, as some projects are likely to slow down. Saturn, Uranus, Neptune and Pluto will all be retrograde, joined by Jupiter from mid-October. This will provide you with the chance to unhook yourself from situations that no longer serve your higher purpose and those you've outgrown.

The partial lunar eclipse and supermoon on 18 September will be in Pisces, and warns that overzealous behaviour and actions you have taken on a whim or based on expectations alone will need correcting at this time. This is all the more reason to ensure the courageous and bold actions you take in 2024 are based on facts, not supposition. If you discover you have made mistakes or obstacles arise, the grand trine between Uranus, Pluto and Mercury at the end of September will be an ideal opportunity to gain ground with your plans.

The final two months of the year may be a frustrating time as both Mercury and Mars will be retrograde. Mercury will be retrograde from 26 November until 15 December. Mars turns retrograde on 6 December.

If you experience a stop-start confusing or frustrating time at the end of the year, look once more at your goals and how you can reach them. If life has been complex or is taking you down a difficult path, the opposition of Mars and Pluto on 3 November could bring things to a head. Luckily, Pluto will provide a boost in motivation after 20 November. The good news will be that if you wish to switch tracks you will very quickly be on a fresh course.

The eclipses in 2024 will be across the Aries–Libra axis, indicating again that the more you can be courageous and take positive action, be dynamic and play a proactive role rather than be passive in your life then the better for you. This will not preclude some projects and plans being tough or challenging but, nevertheless, celestial energy will support your efforts to be independently motivated and proactive.

Look at the Mercury and Mars retrograde periods I've mentioned above for ideal times to reassess, review and, if necessary, take time out.

You will be looking for balance and a fair-play outcome for the many actions you take in 2024, which may seem paradoxical in light of the dynamic approach the year's events will ask you to take. However, sometimes the means to an end are very different to the end you seek, and this is not the time for the end justifying the means.

One motto you may wish to adopt this year is 'Do no harm.'

This is largely because if you adopt a devil-may-care attitude in 2024 the combative aspect of this strong Aries year will lead to aggression, conflict and potentially even strife. This gives added impetus to looking for a practical, structured and relaxed approach that facilitates a determined, action-oriented outcome and the results you want.

The ongoing Neptune–Pluto sextile throughout the year brings opportunities for great personal growth and transformation in your life and will bring relationships and spirituality to a new, inspiring level. Seize the day!

How to use this diary

Solar, lunar and planetary movements

This diary lists the major solar, planetary and lunar movements day by day, and I have interpreted these so you can plan your days, weeks and months according to prevailing astrological trends. You'll gain insight into which days will be favourable for your planned events – from important meetings, get-togethers and celebrations to trips and life decisions – and which days will be variable and even frustrating. You'll see that when you plan your life by the stars sometimes taking ill-timed action can lead to disappointment, and that taking well-timed action will lead to success.

The sun in the zodiac signs

Astrology is the study of the movement of celestial objects from our point of view on Earth. We are most familiar with the study of our sun signs, which depicts the movement and placement of the sun in the zodiac signs Aries through to Pisces. In the same way the sun moves through the zodiac signs Aries to Pisces through the calendar year, so do the planets and other celestial objects such as the centaur Chiron.

This diary features monthly forecasts when the sun is in each sign, beginning with the sun in Capricorn (December 2023 to January 2024) and proceeding through the signs and finishing once again with the sun in Capricorn in December 2024.

Each monthly forecast applies to everyone, as it is a general forecast for all sun signs. There is also a forecast uniquely for your own particular sun sign, so you'll find the 'For Capricorn' section is uniquely for Capricorns and so on. When the sun is in your own sign it can prove particularly motivational and is a great time to get ahead with projects that resonate with your self-esteem, gut instincts and bigger-picture motivation.

The moon in the zodiac signs

Just as the sun moves through the zodiac signs, so does the moon. This diary lists these movements as they can have a perceived influence over the mood and tone of the day, just as the sun in different signs is known to characterise different traits. Where a diary entry states 'The moon enters Taurus', this indicates that the moon has left the zodiac sign Aries and has entered the sign of Taurus and will now reside in Taurus until it moves on to Gemini in a couple of days' time.

New moons and full moons are also listed in this diary, as these can mark turning points within your journey through the year. New moons are generally a great time to begin a new project. Full moons can signify a culmination or a peak in a project or event, so if you're planning to launch a business or your children wish to begin a new course or activity you can check in this diary if the day you're planning your event will be favourable for beginning a fresh venture. Simply check to see if your new venture falls on or near a new moon, and also take a look at the diary entries either side of your proposed events to ensure celestial influences will be working in your favour.

Eclipses can indicate particularly powerful turning points, and it is for this reason eclipses are also listed in the diary dates. If a lunar or solar eclipse is in the same sign as your own particular sun sign it may be particularly potent.

The phases of the moon can truly influence the tone of your day, so this diary features every moon sign for every day. The moon remains in each sign for approximately two days. Below is listed the mood depending on which sign the moon is in on a daily basis.

MOON IN ARIES: can bring an upbeat approach to life, but restlessness or fiery outbursts can result if you or those around you feel they are under pressure.

MOON IN TAURUS: can bring stability to feelings and routine, a sensual time and predilection for all things artistic and musical, but overindulgence and stubbornness can result if you are under pressure.

MOON IN GEMINI: can bring a chatty, talkative approach to life, but flippancy, indecision and uncertainty can result if you or those around you are under pressure.

MOON IN CANCER: a sense of security, nesting, cocooning and nurturance will be sought for family time and those you love, but insecurities or a lack of adaptability can result if you are under pressure.

MOON IN LEO: an upbeat approach to life and a more dynamic attitude to others and yourself will arise, but a Leo moon can bring arrogance, pride and vanity to the surface if you are under pressure.

MOON IN VIRGO: a great time to focus on health, routine, decluttering, work and being helpful, but overanalysis, obsessive attention to detail and ambivalence can also arise if you are under pressure.

MOON IN LIBRA: a lovely time to focus on art, music, love, creating harmony and peace, but a sense of disharmony, indecision and dissatisfaction can arise if you are under pressure.

MOON IN SCORPIO: a time for focusing on personal needs, sensuality, enjoyment of life and indulgence in all things wonderful, but if you are under pressure deep feelings can emerge that are intense or potentially destructive.

MOON IN SAGITTARIUS: an outgoing, upbeat phase when an adventurous attitude will bring out your joviality and lust for learning and life. When you are under pressure, you and others may appear blunt or disregard the feelings of other people.

MOON IN CAPRICORN: this phase can stimulate a practical and focused approach to work and to your goals and plans, but when you are under pressure a sense of limitations, restrictions and authoritarian strictures can arise.

MOON IN AQUARIUS: a quirky, outgoing phase during which trying new activities and new approaches to life will appeal. When you're under pressure the moon in Aquarius may stimulate unreliability, unconventionality or changeability.

MOON IN PISCES: a dreamy, introverted or artistic phase in which music, the arts and romance will thrive. It is also a good time for meditation. When you're under pressure a Pisces moon can bring excessive daydreaming, forgetfulness or vagueness.

NB: if you know your moon sign you may find that when the moon is in your sign, as listed in this diary, life is either easier or more challenging depending on the planetary aspects to your moon at the time of your birth. Keep a note of the general mood or occurrences when the moon is in your sign and you may find that a pattern emerges.

Interplanetary aspects

Astrologers study the movements of planets in relation to each other. The measurements, which are in degrees, minutes and seconds, focus on patterns and particular aspects, which are the angles between the planets, the sun and other celestial objects. This diary includes mention of these aspects between the sun and the planets, and the terminology used is explained below – from 'opposition' (when a planet is opposite another) to 'quincunx' (when a planet is at a 150-degree angle to another).

The angles the planets and the sun make to one another have meanings in astrology. For example, a 'trine' aspect (120-degree angle) can be considered beneficial for the progress of your plans, while a 'square' aspect (90-degree angle) can present as a challenge (depending on your own attitude to challenges and obstacles).

By choosing dates carefully for the fruition of your plans you will be moving forward with the benefit of the knowledge of the cosmic influences that can help your progress.

NB: when you read the planetary aspects in this diary such as 'Sun square Uranus', be aware that the aspect's influence may span to a day before and a day after the actual date it is entered in this diary, especially regarding the outer planets of Neptune, Uranus and Pluto. However, the moon phases are relevant for each day.

Planetary aspects

CONJUNCTION: when a celestial object is at the same degree and generally in the same sign of the zodiac as another celestial object and therefore is aligned from our point of view on Earth. This can intensify the dynamics between celestial objects and Earth.

SEMI-SEXTILE: a 30-degree angle. This is a harmonious aspect or facilitates the flow of energy between planetary influences.

SEXTILE: a 60-degree angle. This can be a peaceful, harmonious influence or it can facilitate the flow of energy between planetary influences.

SQUARE: a 90-degree angle. This can be a challenging aspect, but as some people get going when the going gets tough it can lead to a breakthrough.

TRINE: a 120-degree angle. This can be a peaceful, harmonious influence or facilitate the flow of energy between planetary influences.

QUINCUNX: a 150-degree angle. This can present a hurdle to be overcome.

OPPOSITION: a 180-degree angle, meaning a planet is opposite another. This can intensify the interplanetary dynamics.

Retrogrades

Planets can appear to go backwards from our point of view on Earth. The best-known retrograde phases are those of Mercury and Venus, although all other planets also turn retrograde and these retrograde phases are mentioned in this diary.

Retrograde phases can be a good time to assimilate, consolidate and integrate recent developments, although traditionally retrograde phases are associated with delays or a slow down or a difficult process.

For example, a Mercury retrograde phase is often associated with difficult communications or traffic snarls, yet it can be an excellent time to integrate events and consolidate, review and re-order your ideas. This diary lists the start and finish dates of Mercury retrograde phases, as well as the kinds of activities that may be influenced by this phenomenon.

A 'station' is when planets turn from one direction to the other from our point of view on Earth.

2024 NORTHERN HEMISPHERE MOON PHASES

JANUARY

S	M	T	W	T	F	S
	1	2	3	4	5	6
7	8	9	10	11	12	13
14	15	16	17	18	19	20
21	22	23	24	25	26	27
28	29	30	31			

FEBRUARY

S	M	T	W	T	F	S
				1	2	3
4	5	6	7	8	9	10
11	12	13	14	15	16	17
18	19	20	21	22	23	24
25	26	27	28	29		

MARCH

S	M	T	W	T	F	S
31					1	2
3	4	5	6	7	8	9
10	11	12	13	14	15	16
17	18	19	20	21	22	23
24	25	26	27	28	29	30

APRIL

S	M	T	W	T	F	S
	1	2	3	4	5	6
7	8	9	10	11	12	13
14	15	16	17	18	19	20
21	22	23	24	25	26	27
28	29	30				

MAY

S	M	T	W	T	F	S
			1	2	3	4
5	6	7	8	9	10	11
12	13	14	15	16	17	18
19	20	21	22	23	24	25
26	27	28	29	30	31	

JUNE

S	M	T	W	T	F	S
30						1
2	3	4	5	6	7	8
9	10	11	12	13	14	15
16	17	18	19	20	21	22
23	24	25	26	27	28	29

2024 NORTHERN HEMISPHERE MOON PHASES

JULY

S	M	T	W	T	F	S
	1	2	3	4	5	6
7	8	9	10	11	12	13
14	15	16	17	18	19	20
21	22	23	24	25	26	27
28	29	30	31			

AUGUST

S	M	T	W	T	F	S
				1	2	3
4	5	6	7	8	9	10
11	12	13	14	15	16	17
18	19	20	21	22	23	24
25	26	27	28	29	30	31

SEPTEMBER

S	M	T	W	T	F	S
1	2	3	4	5	6	7
8	9	10	11	12	13	14
15	16	17	18	19	20	21
22	23	24	25	26	27	28
29	30					

OCTOBER

S	M	T	W	T	F	S
		1	2	3	4	5
6	7	8	9	10	11	12
13	14	15	16	17	18	19
20	21	22	23	24	25	26
27	28	29	30	31		

NOVEMBER

S	M	T	W	T	F	S
					1	2
3	4	5	6	7	8	9
10	11	12	13	14	15	16
17	18	19	20	21	22	23
24	25	26	27	28	29	30

DECEMBER

S	M	T	W	T	F	S
1	2	3	4	5	6	7
8	9	10	11	12	13	14
15	16	17	18	19	20	21
22	23	24	25	26	27	28
29	30	31				

○ New moon ● Full moon

January 2024

The sun entered Capricorn, 22 December 2023

Circumstances this New Year's Day will provide a strong indication of how your life is working for you. If you love your New Year's Day then all is well and good, but if not it's time to make changes! Venus in the sign of Sagittarius will help you to be dynamic and goal oriented, encouraging you to make changes in concrete yet optimistic and big-picture ways. Be inspired, but avoid allowing your imagination to run away with you.

Communications may not be the best at the start of the year, so focus on good relationship skills to avoid misunderstandings and mix-ups.

There is a strong indication you will feel escapist, so wait until the Capricorn new moon on 11 January before making rash moves. This new moon will be ideal for taking remedial steps to improve your perspective of your life and the world and to optimise your opportunities to create something substantial for yourself and those you love throughout the year.

Mid-January is a lovely time for socialising and networking. If you're on holiday you're likely to enjoy yourself and being in a beautiful place. If you're working your projects are likely to succeed with due diligence.

As the sun aligns with Pluto from our perspective on Earth on 20-21 January, this is likely to be an intense time. Look at what you can achieve as opposed to what you will lose when you are making important decisions. If you feel you must sacrifice a dream, rest assured you will gain another, much better future as a result. Be aware that you may not be able to see this yet.

For Capricorns

The year begins with a welcome challenge for some Capricorns and with a feeling of tension for others. This exemplifies the two different approaches you can take to the year: the attitude that you can overcome obstacles on the one hand, and the attitude that there will be obstacles or even defeat on the other. The choice is yours, although the first option will pave the way to making life easier.

As Pluto finally leaves your sign after almost two decades, be prepared for developments that will impact considerably on your personal life, especially towards mid-to late January. Beforehand, though, you may realise there are many aspects from your past that need to be resolved – and there is no time like the present.

The more you gain insight into financial and personal agreements the more you can work during the rest of the year towards an abundant life.

The new moon in your own sign on 11 January provides the chance to heal and progress from circumstances that no longer resonate with you. Mars in your sign will contribute to increased energy levels, and a change at home or with family will be a lovely interlude or even a surprise.

INTENTIONS *for the* YEAR

MONDAY 1

Venus square Saturn: what do you want out of 2024, and what will you give to it? This year you can achieve your goals, but giving back to others will be necessary. Moon in Virgo.

TUESDAY 2

Moon in Virgo.

WEDNESDAY 3

Venus quincunx Jupiter: what you want and what someone else wants may be two different things, so find common ground for the best results. Moon in Libra.

THURSDAY 4

Mars enters Capricorn: the following six weeks are ideal for strategising and planning. Moon in Libra.

FRIDAY 5 ☽

Moon in Scorpio.

SATURDAY 6 ☽

Sun square Chiron: someone may ask for your help and you may need to offer someone help. It's a good day for a health appointment but you must be clear about what you want. Avoid taking the remarks of other people personally, unless criticism is merited. Moon in Scorpio.

SUNDAY 7 ☽

Moon enters Sagittarius.

JANUARY

S	M	T	W	T	F	S
	1	2	3	4	5	6
7	8	9	10	11	12	13
14	15	16	17	18	19	20
21	22	23	24	25	26	27
28	29	30	31			

MONDAY 8 ☾

Moon in Sagittarius.

TUESDAY 9 ☾

Mercury square Neptune: avoid misunderstandings and travel delays by being precise and planning ahead. Moon in Sagittarius.

WEDNESDAY 10 ☾

Sun trine Uranus: keep an eye out for a wonderful opportunity. You may hear from someone unexpectedly or receive surprise news. Moon in Capricorn.

THURSDAY 11 ○

New moon in Capricorn; Venus trine Chiron: this is a great day for kick-starting a project and for financial discussions. It's also a good day for a health or beauty appointment. You may be drawn to helping someone. An expert's advice will be useful.

FRIDAY 12

Mars trine Jupiter: take a moment to consider your best strategy and plans and then take action! You'll enjoy meetings and/or news. Avoid overspending. Moon in Aquarius.

SATURDAY 13

Mercury semi-sextile Pluto: it's a good time for a short trip and to make changes in your environment. You may enjoy a lovely talk or get-together. Moon in Aquarius.

SUNDAY 14

Mercury enters Capricorn; Venus quincunx Uranus: the following three weeks are ideal for putting plans in place and for constructive talks. You may be surprised by news or developments, so take things one step at a time. Moon in Pisces.

JANUARY

S	M	T	W	T	F	S
	1	2	3	4	5	6
7	8	9	10	11	12	13
14	15	16	17	18	19	20
21	22	23	24	25	26	27
28	29	30	31			

MONDAY 15   ☽

Moon in Pisces.

TUESDAY 16   ☽

Sun sextile Neptune: you'll enjoy the arts, romance and music, and creative projects will thrive. Avoid forgetfulness; plan ahead! Moon in Aries.

WEDNESDAY 17   ☽

Moon in Aries.

THURSDAY 18   ☽

Mercury sextile Saturn: a lovely day for get-togethers, talks and financial decisions. Moon in Taurus.

FRIDAY 19 ◗

Mercury trine Jupiter; Venus square Neptune: a good day for meetings, a trip and for financial discussions, but you must plan ahead to avoid mix-ups and delays. Moon in Taurus.

SATURDAY 20 ◗

Sun enters Aquarius; sun conjunct Pluto: this may be an intense day, but also a good time to instigate changes if you are not too distracted. Moon enters Gemini.

SUNDAY 21 ●

Pluto enters Aquarius: be prepared to resume new ideas and projects you floated in 2023. Think outside the box for the best results. Moon in Gemini.

JANUARY

S	M	T	W	T	F	S
	1	2	3	4	5	6
7	8	9	10	11	12	13
14	15	16	17	18	19	20
21	22	23	24	25	26	27
28	29	30	31			

January to February 2024

Sun enters Aquarius, 20 January

The conjunction of the sun and Pluto will bring about an intense focus on the new and the different and something also potentially intense as you let go of elements of the past few months. It's an excellent time to get back on track.

In addition, there will be no retrograde planets this zodiacal month, bringing a progressive feeling that is ideal for getting the wind beneath your sails. However, this phase could be detrimental if you feel you've lost your way, which is all the more reason to strive to get on the right track as the astrology of this month will help you.

The Leo full moon on 25 January will spotlight where there is drama in your life at the moment, and will also hold the key to the healthiest way forward. If you like life to be intense and dramatic you'll love this month; if not, you may be well advised to take things carefully to avoid too much intensity and disappointment.

The Aquarian new moon supermoon on 9 February will be particularly useful for putting new plans in place, so if the world or your life seems too stuck on the one hand or too chaotic on the other, make plans for change at this new moon. The days and weeks prior will be ideal for formulating your best approach.

This year's St Valentine's Day will be particularly intense so, again, if you relish drama and intensity you'll love it. If not, find ways to manage emotional highs and lows.

For Aquarians

Long-term change is waiting in the wings, and it'll enter your life whether you want it to or not! The best policy for now will be to improve your skill sets and strengths and minimise weaknesses to ensure you're in the best position to weather any storms.

The news needn't all be bad, however: if you love change and adore feeling you're making waves you'll truly appreciate the doors that open over the next four weeks. Some doors will close simultaneously, so it's vital you decide what you're ready to let go of in your life and what you need to work on a little more before you do.

The full moon in Leo on 25 January may spotlight a particular vulnerability and you'll learn from this how best to navigate ahead, especially in the areas of health, finances, work and your personal life.

There is likely to be intense news and developments early in February, with the chance to move forward aspects that were laid bare in January. The new moon supermoon in your sign on 9 February will be ideal to initiate a fresh chapter in your personal life, especially if it's your birthday, and if you were born mid-February or afterwards at work or in your health life.

A work or personal vulnerability is best approached from a practical point of view. Avoid quick fixes and intense, knee-jerk reactions, especially towards 18 February.

MONDAY 22

Moon enters Cancer.

TUESDAY 23

Venus enters Capricorn: you'll be drawn to a down-to-earth approach to life over the coming two weeks, and this attitude will work for you. Moon in Cancer.

WEDNESDAY 24

Moon in Cancer.

THURSDAY 25

Full moon in Leo; Mars square Chiron: a good time to consider how to approach a thorny topic from a new angle, especially regarding health, study and work.

FRIDAY 26 ●

Mercury square Chiron: a good time to research circumstances, especially regarding health, work and study. Avoid mix-ups and delays by planning ahead. Avoid knocks and scrapes. Moon in Leo.

SATURDAY 27 ●

Sun square Jupiter; Mercury conjunct Mars: avoid making rash decisions and find ways to proceed carefully. You may enjoy a spontaneous get-together. Moon enters Virgo.

SUNDAY 28 ●

Venus sextile Saturn; Mars square moon's nodes: a lovely day for get-togethers and for making agreements. Just avoid being easily influenced and making rash decisions. Moon in Virgo.

JANUARY

S	M	T	W	T	F	S
	1	2	3	4	5	6
7	8	9	10	11	12	13
14	15	16	17	18	19	20
21	22	23	24	25	26	27
28	29	30	31			

MONDAY 29

Mercury trine Uranus; Venus trine Jupiter: you may hear unexpectedly good news or bump into someone. A spontaneous trip may be enjoyable. Finances could progress. Moon in Virgo.

TUESDAY 30

Moon enters Libra.

WEDNESDAY 31

Moon in Libra.

THURSDAY 1

Moon enters Scorpio.

FRIDAY 2 ◐

Mercury sextile Neptune: a good day for meetings and talks. You may also enjoy a romantic, arts-based or creative day. Moon in Scorpio.

SATURDAY 3 ◐

Moon in Scorpio.

SUNDAY 4 ◐

Moon in Sagittarius.

FEBRUARY

S	M	T	W	T	F	S
				1	2	3
4	5	6	7	8	9	10
11	12	13	14	15	16	17
18	19	20	21	22	23	24
25	26	27	28	29		

MONDAY 5   (

Sun sextile Chiron; Mercury conjunct Pluto; Venus square Chiron; Saturn sextile Jupiter: a good time to put plans in action. Financial and personal matters will attract attention, and if you feel overwhelmed ask for expert help. Health may be in the spotlight. Moon in Sagittarius.

TUESDAY 6   (

Venus square moon's nodes: you may need to undertake delicate talks, so be diplomatic. Moon enters Capricorn.

WEDNESDAY 7   (

Venus trine Uranus; Mars sextile Neptune: a good time to promote yourself and your projects and to find ways to get ahead in a most inspired yet constructive way. You may receive unexpectedly good news. Romance could flourish. Moon in Capricorn.

THURSDAY 8   (

Sun square Uranus: be aware that not everyone will agree with your plans and ideas. You may receive unexpected news that causes upheaval. Moon enters Aquarius.

FRIDAY 9 ○

New moon supermoon in Aquarius; Mercury semi-sextile Saturn: a good time to begin something a little quirky and new and for financial decisions, but you must avoid going too left field. You may experience a surprise if you didn't already yesterday.

SATURDAY 10 ☽

Mercury square Jupiter: you may find some communications stall and travel may be delayed, so be patient. Find the time to look for innovative solutions to issues. Moon enters Pisces.

SUNDAY 11 ☽

Moon in Pisces.

FEBRUARY

S	M	T	W	T	F	S
				1	2	3
4	5	6	7	8	9	10
11	12	13	14	15	16	17
18	19	20	21	22	23	24
25	26	27	28	29		

MONDAY 12)

Moon enters Aries.

TUESDAY 13)

Mars enters Aquarius; Venus sextile Neptune: a lovely day for romance, the arts, film and creativity. You may be drawn to trying something new. Moon in Aries.

WEDNESDAY 14)

Mars conjunct Pluto: Happy St Valentine's Day! Strong feelings will emerge, so ensure you maintain perspective. Passion will be intense. Moon enters Taurus.

THURSDAY 15)

Moon in Taurus.

FRIDAY 16 ☽

Venus enters Aquarius: this is a passionate time, especially in the love stakes. Be sure to maintain perspective. Moon enters Gemini.

SATURDAY 17 ☽

Venus conjunct Pluto: romance will appeal and you'll be drawn to spending time with someone you love. Just avoid sensitive topics as these could lead to conflict. Moon in Gemini.

SUNDAY 18 ☽

Moon in Gemini.

FEBRUARY						
S	M	T	W	T	F	S
				1	2	3
4	5	6	7	8	9	10
11	12	13	14	15	16	17
18	19	20	21	22	23	24
25	26	27	28	29		

february to
march 2024

Sun enters Pisces, 19 February

There will again be no planets retrograde this zodiacal month, which will help you to take positive strides ahead with your various plans and projects.

Health and well-being will be a prominent theme now, with Chiron conjunct the moon's north node on 19 February and the Virgo full moon on 24 February providing a strong indication for you about where you are heading with respect to your health and happiness.

In addition, the conjunction of Venus and Mars in Aquarius for most of the zodiacal month will open doors to new ideas and plans and fresh social circles and organisations that will add spice and flavour to your usual routine. It's a great time to be outgoing and willing to meet new people or forums and to research and potentially also to embrace fresh ideas.

While in general this is a good time to be taking action and being optimistic about your plans and projects it's important to avoid impulsiveness, especially at the end of February and on 3 and 9 March.

Romance will be a big drawcard, and you may meet someone you feel a fated connection with. However, if you feel a relationship has run its course this month could see its final demise, especially for Aries,

Librans, Capricorns and Cancerians. If you're not ready to part it's important to find ways to reach common ground, but if you do decide to finally part company be sure to find ways to move forward most amicably to avoid ongoing conflict.

For Pisces

This Pisces season will be inspiring as it will give you the opportunity to imagine a scenario that is both pleasant and something you want, rather than a fantasy. There will be a romantic vibe and the opportunity to dream big, while also anchoring your dreams in reality.

A romantic connection could be inspiring.

Work-wise, you are likely to be drawn to new areas and even to finding fresh ways to work digitally within your existing field more effectively.

A degree of upheaval needn't get in the way of your generally positive progress. Just keep an eye on difficult or unexpected developments that shake up the status quo – be this at work and, for some, in your personal life.

The Virgo full moon on 24 February points to the chance to be more practical about your relationships, both at home and at work, and the Pisces new moon supermoon on 10 March suggests you're ready to reinvent at least one aspect of yourself such as your appearance, daily routine or health schedule.

MONDAY 19 ●

Sun enters Pisces; Chiron conjunct moon's north node: a health matter may require attention. Someone close may ask for your help, and if you need advice or support it will be available. Moon in Cancer.

TUESDAY 20 ●

Moon in Cancer.

WEDNESDAY 21 ●

Moon enters Leo.

THURSDAY 22 ●

Venus conjunct Mars: a good day for get-togethers and for advancing your projects and ideas. Be prepared to look outside the box at options. Moon in Leo.

FRIDAY 23 ●

Mercury enters Pisces: an inspiring three weeks will open your mind to new options and opportunities. Be prepared to discuss your ideas. Moon in Leo.

SATURDAY 24 ●

Full moon in Virgo: consider fresh options and avenues, especially if they provide security and stability while also being meaningful.

SUNDAY 25 ●

Mars semi-sextile Saturn; Mars semi-square Neptune: this is a good time to plan ahead, but you must be realistic and practical. Moon in Virgo.

		FEBRUARY				
S	M	T	W	T	F	S
				1	2	3
4	5	6	7	8	9	10
11	12	13	14	15	16	17
18	19	20	21	22	23	24
25	26	27	28	29		

MONDAY 26 ●

Moon enters Libra.

TUESDAY 27 ●

Mars square Jupiter: while this is a good time in general to take the initiative with your plans and projects, you must avoid impulsive decisions as you may regret them. Moon in Libra.

WEDNESDAY 28 ●

Sun conjunct Mercury; Mercury conjunct Saturn: this is a good day to dream big, but to also keep your feet on the ground! It's a good day to make a commitment. Moon in Libra.

THURSDAY 29 ●

Venus sextile moon's north node: a good day for a get-together and meetings and for gaining direction. Moon in Scorpio.

FRIDAY 1

Sun sextile Jupiter; Mercury semi-sextile Mars; Venus sextile Chiron: an excellent time to make agreements, especially in connection with finances, love, health, long-term projects or travel. Moon in Scorpio.

SATURDAY 2

Moon enters Sagittarius.

SUNDAY 3

Venus square Uranus: you may experience a surprise or unexpected development. Be prepared to think outside the box. Moon in Sagittarius.

MARCH

S	M	T	W	T	F	S
					1	2
3	4	5	6	7	8	9
10	11	12	13	14	15	16
17	18	19	20	21	22	23
24	25	26	27	28	29	30
31						

MONDAY 4 ☾

Moon enters Capricorn.

TUESDAY 5 ☾

Mars sextile moon's north node: a good time for get-togethers and making changes in your health routine. Moon in Capricorn.

WEDNESDAY 6 ☾

Mars sextile Chiron: a good day for a health or beauty appointment. Avoid rushing, impulsiveness and minor bumps and scrapes. Moon in Capricorn.

THURSDAY 7 ☾

Sun semi-sextile Chiron; Mercury semi-sextile Venus: a good day for a health or beauty treat. You can rebuild bridges if you have argued with someone. It's also a good day for get-togethers, negotiations and financial discussions. Romance and a fun event could thrive. Moon in Aquarius.

FRIDAY 8   (

Mercury conjunct Neptune: you'll enjoy a get-together but must avoid sensitive topics. The arts and romance could thrive. Moon in Aquarius.

SATURDAY 9   (

Sun sextile Uranus; sun semi-sextile Mars; Venus semi-sextile Neptune; Mars square Uranus: a busy day for get-togethers, sports, the arts, creativity and romance. Expect a surprise. A circumstance may change quickly. Moon in Pisces.

SUNDAY 10   ○

New moon supermoon in Pisces; Mercury enters Aries; Mercury sextile Pluto: a good day for important discussions and to put new ideas on the table. A get-together could be transformative.

MARCH

S	M	T	W	T	F	S
					1	2
3	4	5	6	7	8	9
10	11	12	13	14	15	16
17	18	19	20	21	22	23
24	25	26	27	28	29	30
31						

MONDAY 11)

Venus enters Pisces: you're likely to be drawn to the arts and a deeper form of self-expression, such as an increasing interest in spirituality, over the coming weeks. Moon in Aries.

TUESDAY 12)

Moon in Aries.

WEDNESDAY 13)

Venus semi-sextile Pluto: a lovely day for get-togethers, although some talks or events may be intense. Moon in Taurus.

THURSDAY 14)

Moon in Taurus.

FRIDAY 15 ❯

Moon in Gemini.

SATURDAY 16 ❯

Mercury semi-sextile Saturn: a good day for meetings and financial planning. Moon in Gemini.

SUNDAY 17 ❯

Sun conjunct Neptune: a lovely day for romance, get-togethers, the arts and music. Moon enters Cancer.

MARCH

S	M	T	W	T	F	S
					1	2
3	4	5	6	7	8	9
10	11	12	13	14	15	16
17	18	19	20	21	22	23
24	25	26	27	28	29	30
31						

March to April 2024

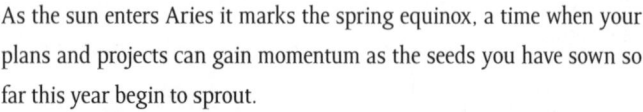

Sun enters Aries, 20 March

As the sun enters Aries it marks the spring equinox, a time when your plans and projects can gain momentum as the seeds you have sown so far this year begin to sprout.

The conjunction of Mercury and Chiron at the end of March will put the focus firmly on health and well-being. It will be an excellent time to recap and review where you are in your health and well-being journey and to get up to date during April so you're in better shape moving forwards.

The annular lunar eclipse in Libra on 25 March will point to an area of your life in which you'll need to find more balance, and this area will be different for everyone. The solar eclipse on 8 April will provide insight into your best path forward.

When Mercury turns retrograde in Aries on 1 April you'll be more inclined to review your progress so far this year, as Mercury retrograde in Aries could really stall developments. Be prepared to get important paperwork and decisions sorted out or at least on the table before 2 April to avoid delays and hindrances and the need to reconfigure some projects already underway during the retrograde period, which lasts until the end of April.

The beginning of April is ideal to focus on romance and the arts and on those people who are truly dear to your heart. Your favourite interests could transform your life at this time.

For Aries

This is your time of year, Aries: a proactive, upbeat time. However, this year you may need to review or revisit some aspects of your life, even if only to ensure you're on track. The lunar eclipse in Libra on 25 March will ask you to consider key relationships first of all, especially if you were born on or before 25 March, and to look at your work, health and daily life from a fresh perspective if you were born later. How can you find more balance in these important arenas?

Mercury turns retrograde in your sign on 1 April, which will slow the pace. You may feel particularly frustrated, so consider how best to use this phase. April will be an ideal time to revisit an old haunt, to focus on updating your health schedule if necessary and also to resume contact with people you have lost touch with. Early April is also an ideal time to let your interests flourish in self-development, well-being and spirituality.

The total solar eclipse in your sign on 8 April signals a fresh chapter in your personal life if you were born on or before this date, and a fresh work or health regime if you were born later. Be prepared to innovate. A friend or organisation may be helpful, so aim to seek advice or embrace collaborations.

MONDAY 18

Moon in Cancer.

TUESDAY 19

Mars semi-sextile Neptune: a good time to consider how to improve or beautify an area of your life and to take action to make it happen. Moon enters Leo.

WEDNESDAY 20

Sun enters Aries; Mercury conjunct Chiron; spring equinox: this is a period of growth and a good time to take the initiative with your ideas and plans. It's a good day for a health appointment and to build bridges. Moon in Leo.

THURSDAY 21

Sun sextile Pluto; Venus conjunct Saturn: a good time to make changes, agreements and financial arrangements. Moon in Leo.

FRIDAY 22 ●

Mars enters Pisces: the next five weeks will be ideal to infuse a little inspiration into your activities to liven up your life! Just avoid being easily distracted and forgetful. Moon in Virgo.

SATURDAY 23 ●

Jupiter semi-sextile moon's north node: there will be a learning opportunity. You may meet someone influential or someone who seems strangely familiar, even if you've never met before. Moon in Virgo.

SUNDAY 24 ●

Moon enters Libra.

MARCH

S	M	T	W	T	F	S
					1	2
3	4	5	6	7	8	9
10	11	12	13	14	15	16
17	18	19	20	21	22	23
24	25	26	27	28	29	30
31						

MONDAY 25 ●

Lunar eclipse in Libra; Mars semi-sextile Pluto: a relationship matter may come to a head. It's a lovely day to be proactive and get things done. Moon in Libra.

TUESDAY 26 ●

Venus semi-sextile Chiron: a good day for a health or beauty treat and also for overcoming differences. Moon in Libra.

WEDNESDAY 27 ●

Moon enters Scorpio.

THURSDAY 28 ●

Venus sextile Uranus: a good day for meetings and for trying something new. You may hear unexpected news. Moon in Scorpio.

FRIDAY 29

Moon enters Sagittarius.

SATURDAY 30

Moon in Sagittarius.

SUNDAY 31

Moon in Sagittarius.

MARCH						
S	M	T	W	T	F	S
					1	2
3	4	5	6	7	8	9
10	11	12	13	14	15	16
17	18	19	20	21	22	23
24	25	26	27	28	29	30
31						

MONDAY 1 ◖

Mercury turns retrograde: you may receive key news that helps you better understand someone or a project. You'll gain the opportunity to review and rectify any problems over the coming three to four weeks. Moon in Capricorn.

TUESDAY 2 ◖

Moon in Capricorn.

WEDNESDAY 3 ◖

Venus conjunct Neptune: a wonderful day for romance, although you may also tend to be a little head in the clouds. If you're working you'll need to focus. Moon in Aquarius.

THURSDAY 4 ◖

Sun conjunct moon's north node: a good day for meetings. You may encounter someone who can really help move along a project for you. Moon in Aquarius.

FRIDAY 5   (

Venus enters Aries: a more proactive and dynamic phase romantically is about to begin. Be bold! Moon in Pisces.

SATURDAY 6   (

Venus sextile Pluto: a good day to make changes in an important area of your life. Moon in Pisces.

SUNDAY 7   (

Moon enters Aries.

APRIL

S	M	T	W	T	F	S
	1	2	3	4	5	6
7	8	9	10	11	12	13
14	15	16	17	18	19	20
21	22	23	24	25	26	27
28	29	30				

MONDAY 8 ○

Total solar eclipse in Aries; sun conjunct Chiron; sun semi-sextile Jupiter: there is a healing tone about this eclipse, as it aligns with Chiron. Take positive action to accomplish goals, especially those related to health.

TUESDAY 9 ◗

Moon enters Taurus.

WEDNESDAY 10 ◗

Sun semi-sextile Uranus; Mars conjunct Saturn: this is a good day to make agreements and arrangements and for get-togethers at work, socially and at home. You may experience a pleasant surprise. Moon in Taurus.

THURSDAY 11 ◗

Sun conjunct Mercury: another lovely day for get-togethers and to review paperwork and contracts and return to an old haunt. Moon enters Gemini.

FRIDAY 12 ☽

Moon in Gemini.

SATURDAY 13 ☽

Moon enters Cancer.

SUNDAY 14 ☽

Moon in Cancer.

APRIL

S	M	T	W	T	F	S
	1	2	3	4	5	6
7	8	9	10	11	12	13
14	15	16	17	18	19	20
21	22	23	24	25	26	27
28	29	30				

MONDAY 15 ◗

Mercury conjunct Chiron: a good day for a health or beauty appointment. You may be drawn to improving communications or transport by updating a device or vehicle. Moon in Cancer.

TUESDAY 16 ◗

Mars semi-sextile Chiron: a good day to improve health and well-being. Avoid rushing, as minor scrapes and accidents may arise. Moon in Leo.

WEDNESDAY 17 ◗

Venus conjunct moon's north node: a good day for romance and for a meeting with an expert. Moon in Leo.

THURSDAY 18 ◗

Moon enters Virgo.

FRIDAY 19 ●

Sun enters Taurus; Mercury conjunct Venus; Mars sextile Jupiter and Uranus: this is a lovely day for a reunion. You may hear unexpected news. It's also a good time to review your health and well-being program. Moon in Virgo.

SATURDAY 20 ●

Moon in Virgo.

SUNDAY 21 ●

Sun square Pluto; Venus conjunct Chiron; Jupiter conjunct Uranus: expect important or intense developments that will spell changes, some of which may be unexpected. Be prepared to think in the long term and put your health first. Moon enters Libra.

APRIL

S	M	T	W	T	F	S
	1	2	3	4	5	6
7	8	9	10	11	12	13
14	15	16	17	18	19	20
21	22	23	24	25	26	27
28	29	30				

April to May 2024

Sun enters Taurus, 19 April

This is an excellent time to get up to date with your health practices. You're likely to receive news to do with health at the time of the sun's entry into Taurus. Some news may be unexpected, but it will give you a kick-start to improve your daily health schedule.

The conjunction of Jupiter and Uranus on 21 April is bound to bring a surprise or two your way. It's a good time to take plans and projects to the next level, but you must avoid pushing projects that are not yet ready to be implemented. The concurrent tough angle between the sun and Pluto could bring out intense emotions and the conjunction of Chiron and Venus a plethora of health or anxiety issues, so tread carefully during this time.

The Scorpio full moon on 24 April will be a good time to reinvigorate various ideas and plans. Mercury will end its retrograde phase on 25 April and may bring key news your way from someone important. Be prepared to consider how to improve your communications and relationships, such as reconfiguring or updating a device or transport route or even updating a vehicle.

It will take a few weeks to get communications back on an even keel, so avoid feeling that everything will fall into place on or shortly after 25 April at the end of the Mercury retrograde phase. However, the good news is that you'll get the time to rearrange important matters in the meantime.

For Taureans

The conjunction of Jupiter and Uranus in your sign on 21 April will present fresh options and opportunities, some of which will be more challenging than others. A focus on health and well-being plus an eye on long-term goals will be priorities.

It's time for something new, and the spirit of adventure and entrepreneurship will appeal. You may be super lucky and experience a breakthrough at work; if you were born in mid-May you'll experience considerable changes in your personal life.

The full moon in Scorpio on 24 April will mark the culmination of a work or health circumstance, bringing you the opportunity to reinvent your daily routine.

The new moon in your sign on 8 May will offer the chance to make solid agreements and arrangements that can offer you more stability and security moving forward. Luckily, Mercury will contribute to improved communications as May progresses, enabling you to configure a more suitable daily and health routine, so be sure to place your attention on these areas.

MONDAY 22 ●

Venus semi-sextile Uranus: you may enjoy a spontaneous get-together or good news. Moon in Libra.

TUESDAY 23 ●

Moon enters Scorpio.

WEDNESDAY 24 ●

Full moon in Scorpio; Mercury semi-sextile Saturn: this full moon will spotlight where in your life you could bring more of a sense of stability. It's a good day to discuss financial and personal plans for the future.

THURSDAY 25 ●

Mercury ends its retrograde phase: you may receive key news or enjoy a trip. Communications will begin to feel more dynamic over the coming days and weeks. Moon in Scorpio.

FRIDAY 26 ●

Moon in Sagittarius.

SATURDAY 27 ●

Moon in Sagittarius.

SUNDAY 28 ◗

Venus semi-sextile Neptune: a lovely day for romance and the arts and to relax. Moon enters Capricorn.

APRIL

S	M	T	W	T	F	S
	1	2	3	4	5	6
7	8	9	10	11	12	13
14	15	16	17	18	19	20
21	22	23	24	25	26	27
28	29	30				

MONDAY 29 ◖

Venus enters Taurus; Mars conjunct Neptune: romance could go off the dial, but this is also a time to gain a more earthed and grounded appreciation of circumstances. Avoid intense discussions over the coming days as these could escalate. Moon in Capricorn.

TUESDAY 30 ◖

Mars enters Aries: the next few weeks will be ideal for getting things done. You'll appreciate a sense of increased potential for positive outcomes but must avoid feeling frustrated by delays. Moon enters Aquarius.

WEDNESDAY 1 ◖

Venus square Pluto: intense emotions may arise, either yours or someone else's, so the calmer you can be through your day the better it will be for you. Moon in Aquarius.

THURSDAY 2 ◖

Pluto turns retrograde: another intense day when taking things carefully will avoid emotional and potentially destructive interactions. Moon enters Pisces.

FRIDAY 3   (

Mars sextile Pluto: a good day to get on top of projects and recent changes but also to avoid conflict, as difficult or explosive situations could arise. You'll enjoy a get-together and can improve your circumstances. Moon in Pisces.

SATURDAY 4   (

Moon enters Aries.

SUNDAY 5   (

Sun semi-sextile moon's north node: you'll enjoy get-togethers and doing what you love to do. Moon in Aries.

MAY

S	M	T	W	T	F	S
			1	2	3	4
5	6	7	8	9	10	11
12	13	14	15	16	17	18
19	20	21	22	23	24	25
26	27	28	29	30	31	

MONDAY 6 (

Saturn semi-square Pluto: you may experience a little Mondayitis but will soon get into the flow of things and could excel as a result. Moon enters Taurus.

TUESDAY 7 (

Sun sextile Saturn; Mercury conjunct Chiron: a good day for get-togethers and business meetings and for boosting your health and well-being. An expert may be particularly helpful. Moon in Taurus.

WEDNESDAY 8 ○

New moon in Taurus: you may experience a surprise at this new moon. It's excellent for beginning something a bit different, such as a fresh study course.

THURSDAY 9)

Moon in Gemini.

FRIDAY 10)

Moon in Gemini.

SATURDAY 11)

Sun semi-sextile Chiron; Venus semi-sextile moon's north node: a lovely day for get-togethers and romance. A health or beauty treat may appeal. Moon in Cancer.

SUNDAY 12)

Moon in Cancer.

MAY						
S	M	T	W	T	F	S
			1	2	3	4
5	6	7	8	9	10	11
12	13	14	15	16	17	18
19	20	21	22	23	24	25
26	27	28	29	30	31	

MONDAY 13 ❯

Sun conjunct Uranus; Venus sextile Saturn: a good day to be outspoken and dynamic and to make agreements, especially financially, if you've done your research. Moon enters Leo.

TUESDAY 14 ❯

Moon in Leo.

WEDNESDAY 15 ❯

Mercury enters Taurus: a grounded, earthy approach to communications and relationships will work well over the coming three weeks. Moon enters Virgo.

THURSDAY 16 ❯

Moon in Virgo.

FRIDAY 17

Mercury square Pluto; Mars semi-square Jupiter: misunderstandings and traffic delays are likely, so be prepared to plan ahead. It's a good day to avoid making rash decisions, as these could backfire. Moon in Virgo.

SATURDAY 18

Sun conjunct Jupiter; Venus conjunct Uranus: expect unanticipated developments or meetings. You may be pleasantly surprised, but if not look for ways to find common ground and avoid arguments. Moon enters Libra.

SUNDAY 19

Sun sextile Neptune: a lovely day for romance, the arts and generally relaxing. Moon in Libra.

MAY

S	M	T	W	T	F	S
			1	2	3	4
5	6	7	8	9	10	11
12	13	14	15	16	17	18
19	20	21	22	23	24	25
26	27	28	29	30	31	

May to June 2024

Sun enters Gemini, 20 May

As the sun enters Gemini it makes a harmonious aspect with powerful and transformative Pluto, providing the opportunity to make positive change in your life. There is so much potential in this zodiacal month, and it is excellent for improving communication skills and therefore also both business and personal relationships.

Venus and subsequently Jupiter will harmoniously aspect Pluto, bringing the opportunity for long-lasting change. If you already have plans and projects in the making this is an excellent time to put them in motion, as they are likely to succeed.

However, if you have felt a little fatalistic about life and have let life run its own course, it's likely events will continue to gain their own momentum. If there are aspects of your life you don't like, it's important to change them before they take you somewhere you don't want to be.

Mercury joins the sun, Venus and Jupiter in Gemini on 3 June, bringing the focus squarely on communications and long-term plans and the chance to develop favourite projects and ideas.

As Mars enters Taurus on 9 June it will be important to channel restlessness into productive activities to avoid frustrations getting the better of you over the following few weeks.

A couple of tough situations could become obstacles you dislike, especially from 7 to 13 June, but if you work hard at your goals even if you seem to encounter obstacles you will make a breakthrough, perhaps even in unexpected ways.

For Geminis

This is a very go-ahead time for you. Be positive, as so much can go right. The full moon on 23 May will spotlight where luck lies with you, and where you may need to make a course correction.

The entry of Jupiter into Gemini on 26 May will put your focus squarely on a close relationship. If you are single, the upcoming 12 months will be ideal for finding good company.

Early June is a particularly lovely time for get-togethers and for travel, and for transforming important aspects of your life such as the areas in which you share responsibilities.

The new moon on 6 June could revitalise your life, especially if it's your birthday. Someone close will factor into your plans and romance could truly lift off. If you are single this is a good time to take the initiative to find someone compatible.

Two days after the new moon, important decisions will be on the table. If you encounter obstacles find practical, reasonable and long-term solutions, particularly with someone special in your life or a collaborator at work.

MONDAY 20 ●

Sun enters Gemini; Mars conjunct moon's north node: there will be an unavoidable meeting or development. Be proactive, but avoid making rash decisions that could backfire. Moon enters Scorpio.

TUESDAY 21 ●

Moon in Scorpio.

WEDNESDAY 22 ●

Sun trine Pluto: an excellent time to make changes, and if developments assume their own positive momentum to work along with events. Moon in Scorpio.

THURSDAY 23 ●

Full moon in Sagittarius; Venus enters Gemini; Venus conjunct Jupiter; Jupiter sextile Neptune: a time of great potential, when good partnerships and agreements can be forged. Romance could blossom too! Be adventurous.

FRIDAY 24 ●

Moon in Sagittarius.

SATURDAY 25 ●

Venus trine Pluto: a lovely weekend for romance and the arts, film and creativity. Moon in Capricorn.

SUNDAY 26 ●

Jupiter enters Gemini: a fresh one-year phase when communications and relationships will take key focus in your life. Moon in Capricorn.

MAY						
S	M	T	W	T	F	S
			1	2	3	4
5	6	7	8	9	10	11
12	13	14	15	16	17	18
19	20	21	22	23	24	25
26	27	28	29	30	31	

MONDAY 27

Moon enters Aquarius.

TUESDAY 28

Mercury sextile Saturn: a good day for talks, meetings, planning and financial discussions. Moon in Aquarius.

WEDNESDAY 29

Mars conjunct Chiron: a good day for a health appointment. You must avoid rushing as mistakes can be made. An expert's advice may be necessary. Moon in Aquarius.

THURSDAY 30

Mercury semi-sextile Mars and Chiron: another good day to focus on health and well-being and to seek help from an expert. Your help may be required. Moon in Pisces.

FRIDAY 31 ☽

Moon in Pisces.

SATURDAY 1 ☽

Mars semi-sextile Uranus: you'll enjoy an impromptu event or doing something different. Just avoid making rash decisions. Moon in Aries.

SUNDAY 2 ☽

Moon in Aries.

JUNE

S	M	T	W	T	F	S
						1
2	3	4	5	6	7	8
9	10	11	12	13	14	15
16	17	18	19	20	21	22
23	24	25	26	27	28	29
30						

JUNE

MONDAY 3   (

*Mercury enters Gemini; Jupiter trine Pluto: an excellent time to make changes
that will have a long-term effect. Moon in Taurus.*

TUESDAY 4   (

*Sun conjunct Venus; Mercury conjunct Jupiter; sun and Venus sextile moon's
north node: a lovely day for meetings, travel and self-improvement. Romance
could also blossom. Moon in Taurus.*

WEDNESDAY 5   (

Moon in Gemini.

THURSDAY 6   ○

*New moon in Gemini: this new moon is conjunct Venus and promises to bring
love and money centre stage as you prepare for a fresh chapter. Be prepared to
think logically to avoid idealism.*

FRIDAY 7)

Moon in Cancer.

SATURDAY 8)

Venus square Saturn; Mars semi-sextile Neptune: an opportunity to think carefully and to be practical about your plans. Avoid limiting your options but, equally, be prepared to be optimistic without engaging in overt idealism. Moon in Cancer.

SUNDAY 9)

Sun square Saturn; Mars enters Taurus: once again, aim to be realistic as some negotiations and talks may be tough. Be prepared to listen and to come to mutually agreeable solutions to problems. Moon enters Leo.

JUNE

S	M	T	W	T	F	S
						1
2	3	4	5	6	7	8
9	10	11	12	13	14	15
16	17	18	19	20	21	22
23	24	25	26	27	28	29
30						

MONDAY 10   )

Moon in Leo.

TUESDAY 11   )

Venus sextile Chiron: a healing day on which you can find common ground with someone special, especially if you've argued. Just avoid sensitive topics and be tactful. Moon in Leo.

WEDNESDAY 12   )

Mercury square Saturn: a good day to be tactful and diplomatic as otherwise someone could take offence over rash words. Avoid misunderstandings and plan extra time for travel. Moon in Virgo.

THURSDAY 13   )

Venus semi-sextile Uranus: you'll enjoy doing something different and may hear unexpectedly good news. Moon in Virgo.

FRIDAY 14 ◗

Sun conjunct Mercury: a trip or meeting is likely to catch your attention. It's a good day for get-togethers and a short trip, although you may also experience a surprise. Moon enters Libra.

SATURDAY 15 ◗

Sun semi-sextile Uranus: you'll enjoy an impromptu event and a change of routine or circumstance. You may be surprised by news. Moon in Libra.

SUNDAY 16 ●

Moon in Libra.

JUNE						
S	M	T	W	T	F	S
						1
2	3	4	5	6	7	8
9	10	11	12	13	14	15
16	17	18	19	20	21	22
23	24	25	26	27	28	29
30						

MONDAY 17 ●

Mercury and Venus enter Cancer; Mercury conjunct Venus; Mercury and Venus square Neptune: you'll hear key news that could put a new slant on a circumstance or relationship. Misunderstandings and mysteries will be prevalent, so take things one step at a time. Moon in Scorpio.

TUESDAY 18 ●

Moon in Scorpio.

WEDNESDAY 19 ●

Moon enters Sagittarius.

THURSDAY 20 ●

Sun enters Cancer; sun square Neptune: take developments as signposts for the best way forward. If your path is blocked, trust your intuition and look for ways you can nurture yourself and others. Moon in Sagittarius.

FRIDAY 21 ●

Mercury sextile Mars: take a moment to get together with like-minded people; you'll be glad you did! Moon in Sagittarius.

SATURDAY 22 ●

Full moon in Capricorn; sun quincunx Pluto; Venus semi-sextile Jupiter: this is a good time for get-togethers and to find your feet and earth your projects and ideas. Romance could also blossom. A trip may appeal. Avoid overindulgence and arguments, as you'll regret it tomorrow.

SUNDAY 23 ●

Mercury square moon's nodes: decide on and communicate your priorities carefully to avoid upsets. Moon in Capricorn.

JUNE

S	M	T	W	T	F	S
						1
2	3	4	5	6	7	8
9	10	11	12	13	14	15
16	17	18	19	20	21	22
23	24	25	26	27	28	29
30						

June to July 2024

Sun enters Cancer, 20 June

When the sun enters Cancer it marks the summer solstice in the northern hemisphere. The day is the longest, and our minds turn to the harvest time arriving soon. It is a period when your activities may peak and you realise the importance of self-nurture and nurturance of others so that you attain your greatest collective potential. You may consider how far you've come already this year and which areas of your life you might like to develop more.

The two Capricorn full moons, one just two days after the summer solstice and the second on 21 July, will illuminate where in your life you are best to take things slowly and build a strong platform both for yourself and those you care for such as friends and family.

Early July will be an excellent time to make a commitment to someone or a project. However, it's important to be discerning at this time and to be careful about who you venture into collaborations and agreements with. Trust your intuition and do your due research before making key commitments.

Keep an eye out for unexpected developments in mid-July. Take extra time for travel and avoid making rash decisions, as minor accidents and complications could occur. For many, though, unexpected developments could open doors to exciting change, so be positive while also being aware that hasty actions are generally regrettable.

For Cancerians

You're known for your nurturing abilities, and with the sun joined by Venus and Mercury in your sign for most of this zodiacal month you'll appreciate the opportunity to focus on your nurturing skills. However, you are likely to need to choose between which activities, values and even people you prioritise now.

The two full moons in Capricorn, one on 22 June and the second on 21 July, will spotlight where you can let go of some of the values and principles you've outgrown, as new ideas and ethics will take their place. You may begin a fresh financial phase or see a relationship in a different light.

The end of June will be a wonderful time for get-togethers, meetings and travel, either involving a favourite project or someone special. Just avoid assuming that someone special is on the same page as you to avoid misunderstandings.

July's flavour includes equal amounts of positive opportunities as pitfalls. Once Mercury leaves your sign on 2 July you're going to be prone to being overly optimistic, which on one hand is good for getting things done but on the other could lead to rash decision-making.

The new moon in Cancer on 5 July is a case in point: you'll feel drawn to something new and even quirky and exciting, but must consider the variables and the actual repercussions of your actions as opposed to simply following the dream. Once you do you may discover that being grounded and practical has its own set of miracles!

MONDAY 24 ●

Moon in Aquarius.

TUESDAY 25 ●

Mars semi-sextile moon's north node: you may be restless or drawn to connecting with someone. Just avoid making rash decisions you will come to regret. Moon in Aquarius.

WEDNESDAY 26 ◖

Mercury trine Saturn; Venus square moon's north node: it's a good day for discussions and financial decisions. Avoid making assumptions; however, if you experience a little tension with someone close, take steps to establish common ground if possible. Moon in Pisces.

THURSDAY 27 ◖

Moon in Pisces.

FRIDAY 28 ◖

Mercury square Chiron: you may need to attend to health and well-being matters. You must avoid rushing and minor accidents and misunderstandings. Moon enters Aries.

SATURDAY 29 ◖

Venus sextile Mars: this is a lovely day for meetings, discussions, romance, the arts and creativity, so take the initiative! Moon in Aries.

SUNDAY 30 ◖

Mercury sextile Uranus: you'll enjoy an impromptu visit or trip and being spontaneous. You may experience a surprise. Moon enters Taurus.

JUNE

S	M	T	W	T	F	S
						1
2	3	4	5	6	7	8
9	10	11	12	13	14	15
16	17	18	19	20	21	22
23	24	25	26	27	28	29
30						

MONDAY 1   (

Moon in Taurus.

TUESDAY 2   (

Mercury enters Leo; Neptune turns retrograde; sun square moon's north node; Mercury trine Neptune: double-check your projects are on the right track. Trust your intuition. Moon enters Gemini.

WEDNESDAY 3   (

Mercury opposite Pluto; Venus trine Saturn: this is an excellent day to initiate financial and personal discussions, and if you're already close to making an arrangement to make an agreement or commitment. Avoid power struggles. Moon in Gemini.

THURSDAY 4   (

Moon enters Cancer.

FRIDAY 5 ○

New moon in Cancer; Mars sextile Saturn: an excellent time to kick-start a new self-nurturing phase, where looking after yourself and your health and well-being come first. As a result you'll be able to look after others better. It's a good day to be industrious, as your efforts will be worthwhile.

SATURDAY 6)

Venus square Chiron: you may feel sensitive, so keep an eye on your emotions. Avoid taking the comments of other people personally, unless criticism is merited. Moon in Cancer.

SUNDAY 7)

Moon in Leo.

JULY

S	M	T	W	T	F	S
	1	2	3	4	5	6
7	8	9	10	11	12	13
14	15	16	17	18	19	20
21	22	23	24	25	26	27
28	29	30	31			

MONDAY 8)

Mercury trine moon's north node; Venus sextile Uranus: an unexpected development could put you in a better place. Keep an eye out for opportunities so you can enjoy life more. You may meet someone you like or admire. Moon in Leo.

TUESDAY 9)

Moon enters Virgo.

WEDNESDAY 10)

Moon in Virgo.

THURSDAY 11)

Venus enters Leo; sun trine Saturn; Venus trine Neptune; Mars semi-sextile Chiron: a good day to work constructively towards your goals. It's also a good day for health and well-being appointments. Moon in Virgo.

FRIDAY 12 ☽

Venus opposite Pluto: this may be an intense day; either you or someone close may be emotional. Romance and passions could soar. Moon in Libra.

SATURDAY 13 ☽

Moon in Libra.

SUNDAY 14 ☽

Moon enters Scorpio.

JULY

S	M	T	W	T	F	S
	1	2	3	4	5	6
7	8	9	10	11	12	13
14	15	16	17	18	19	20
21	22	23	24	25	26	27
28	29	30	31			

MONDAY 15   ●

*Sun square Chiron; Mars conjunct Uranus: you or someone close may feel
a little sensitive, so take things one step at a time. Avoid rushing, minor
accidents, bumps and scrapes. A surprise is on the way. Moon in Scorpio.*

TUESDAY 16   ●

Moon in Scorpio.

WEDNESDAY 17   ●

Moon in Sagittarius.

THURSDAY 18   ●

*Sun sextile Uranus: you'll enjoy a surprise or unexpected development.
Take the initiative, as you'll enjoy doing something out of the ordinary.
Moon in Sagittarius.*

FRIDAY 19 ●

Mercury trine Chiron; Venus trine moon's north node: a lovely day to get together with someone special. It's also a good day for progressive talks and visits somewhere healing. Moon in Capricorn.

SATURDAY 20 ●

Mars enters Gemini: you may receive key news or take a trip somewhere new. You'll enjoy socialising. Moon in Capricorn.

SUNDAY 21 ●

Full moon in Capricorn; Mercury square Uranus; Venus sextile Jupiter: another good day for socialising. You could build a strong relationship with someone. However, misunderstandings and unexpected developments are likely so clear the air first. Moon enters Aquarius.

JULY

S	M	T	W	T	F	S
	1	2	3	4	5	6
7	8	9	10	11	12	13
14	15	16	17	18	19	20
21	22	23	24	25	26	27
28	29	30	31			

July to August 2024

Sun enters Leo, 22 July

There is a dreamy, optimistic, spiritual and creative vibe in the air. You may even need to pinch yourself: is all that is happening real, and are you really on track or is it all in your mind? It's an excellent time to ground yourself and carry out a progress check.

There is every chance you'll undergo a transformative month, but in the process you must avoid power struggles and mix-ups as these could set you back immeasurably.

The Leo new moon on 4 August will be ideal for beginning fresh and adventurous projects and incentives, but you must be sure to have researched these thoroughly before you begin and to avoid idealism and unrealistic expectations.

Try to get important paperwork and decisions on the table, at least, before Mercury turns retrograde on 5 August, as you will subsequently avoid having to rethink your plans. The Mercury retrograde phase until 29 August will be ideal for getting back on track if you feel you have missed a beat, and to reconsider strategies or goals.

Be careful with decisions in mid-August, especially those that will have long-term repercussions and to do with finances.

The full moon in Aquarius on 19 August will be a powerful time. Events will spotlight personal and financial matters, so be sure to do your research beforehand as matters are likely to come to a head at this time. The issue will revolve around where it is best to invest your time and energy. Decide carefully. Mercury is still retrograde, so be sure to research circumstances and take your time if possible before making decisions.

For Leos

The next few weeks could be transformative, especially if you were born at the end of July, although all Leos will benefit from the option of making serious or long-term changes to your daily schedule, health and well-being. You may also need to decide whether a particular group or organisation is the right one for you.

The Leo new moon on 4 August will spotlight where you will benefit from more focus on your work life and health if you were born after 4 August, and if you were born before then how you are best to proceed in your personal life.

Mercury turns retrograde on 5 August and will help you to decipher over the next few weeks where your true loyalties lie.

As it will also be in your money zone, this Mercury retrograde phase will be a good time to reconsider how you budget and manage your investments.

The full moon in Aquarius on 19 August will spotlight in which areas you are ready to move ahead and change your daily schedule, perhaps even in a quirky way.

MONDAY 22 ●

Sun enters Leo; Mars trine Pluto: a good time to move ahead with your plans and projects. Be bold but avoid conflict, as it could be long-standing. Avoid mix-ups and travel delays by planning ahead. Moon in Aquarius.

TUESDAY 23 ●

Sun opposite Pluto: you may be surprised by your own effectiveness and abilities, but you must avoid power struggles. Equally, you must avoid giving your power away. Moon enters Pisces.

WEDNESDAY 24 ●

Moon in Pisces.

THURSDAY 25 ◗

Mercury enters Virgo; Mercury quincunx Neptune: take a moment to double-check you're on track. Avoid mix-ups and misunderstandings. Moon enters Aries.

FRIDAY 26 ◖

*Sun sextile Mars: this is a productive day, but you must avoid cutting corners.
Moon in Aries.*

SATURDAY 27 ◖

*Mercury quincunx Pluto; Venus quincunx Saturn: you may enter into a power
play yet this could cause obstacles. Consider less stressful ways to overcome
relationship issues. Moon enters Taurus.*

SUNDAY 28 ◖

Moon in Taurus.

JULY

S	M	T	W	T	F	S
	1	2	3	4	5	6
7	8	9	10	11	12	13
14	15	16	17	18	19	20
21	22	23	24	25	26	27
28	29	30	31			

MONDAY 29   ❨

Moon enters Gemini.

TUESDAY 30   ❨

Venus trine Chiron: a healing day ideal for a health or beauty treat.
Moon in Gemini.

WEDNESDAY 31   ❨

Sun trine moon's north node: you'll enjoy getting together with someone who
has a beneficial effect on you, such as an expert, adviser or someone you love or
admire. Moon in Gemini.

THURSDAY 1   ❨

Moon in Cancer.

FRIDAY 2   (

Venus square Uranus; Mars sextile moon's north node: expect an unusual event. Avoid taking other people's actions personally, unless you're asked to find a solution. Moon in Cancer.

SATURDAY 3   (

Moon enters Leo.

SUNDAY 4   ○

New moon in Leo; Venus quincunx Neptune: this is a good time to consider where your strengths lie and to take action accordingly. Avoid making assumptions, and get key paperwork and decisions sorted before tomorrow if possible.

AUGUST

S	M	T	W	T	F	S
				1	2	3
4	5	6	7	8	9	10
11	12	13	14	15	16	17
18	19	20	21	22	23	24
25	26	27	28	29	30	31

MONDAY 5)

Mercury turns retrograde; Venus enters Virgo; Venus quincunx Pluto: it's a good time to be precise and discerning about your decisions, the people you mix with and your agreements. Avoid power struggles as these could become long-standing. Moon enters Virgo.

TUESDAY 6)

Moon in Virgo.

WEDNESDAY 7)

Sun sextile Jupiter: a relatively lucky day, but you must avoid both financial and emotional gambling. Moon in Virgo.

THURSDAY 8)

Mercury conjunct Venus: you may enjoy a reunion and news from the past. It's a good time for a work or health review. Moon enters Libra.

FRIDAY 9　　　　　　　　　　　　　　　　　　　　❭

Moon in Libra.

SATURDAY 10　　　　　　　　　　　　　　　　　　❭

Sun quincunx Saturn: a good day to clear chores and be clever about overcoming conundrums, because as a result you will do just that. Moon enters Scorpio.

SUNDAY 11　　　　　　　　　　　　　　　　　　　❭

Moon in Scorpio.

AUGUST

S	M	T	W	T	F	S
				1	2	3
4	5	6	7	8	9	10
11	12	13	14	15	16	17
18	19	20	21	22	23	24
25	26	27	28	29	30	31

MONDAY 12 ◗

Moon in Scorpio.

TUESDAY 13 ◗

Moon in Sagittarius.

WEDNESDAY 14 ●

Mercury quincunx Pluto; Mars conjunct Jupiter: matters you had on the table for discussion at the end of July are likely to resurface. It's a good time to find a progressive solution to problems. This is likely to be a busy or tense day so avoid taking on too much and making rash decisions, especially financial ones. Moon in Sagittarius.

THURSDAY 15 ●

Sun trine Chiron; Mercury quincunx Neptune: ensure you have all the details before making commitments or financial arrangements. A good day for a health consultation. Moon enters Capricorn.

FRIDAY 16 ●

Mars square Saturn: this is a good day to be careful with your various decisions as you could make progress, but you must avoid making rash choices and minor bumps and scrapes. Moon in Capricorn.

SATURDAY 17 ●

Moon enters Aquarius.

SUNDAY 18 ●

Mercury square Uranus: a surprise development needn't derail your whole day. Avoid misunderstandings and traffic delays by planning ahead. Moon in Aquarius.

AUGUST						
S	M	T	W	T	F	S
				1	2	3
4	5	6	7	8	9	10
11	12	13	14	15	16	17
18	19	20	21	22	23	24
25	26	27	28	29	30	31

August to september 2024

Sun enters Virgo, 22 August

Consider this: what is complex in your life, and what obstacles can you overcome so you can move ahead? A tough angle between Venus and Mars indicates you may not get the outcome or agreement you want unless you're careful, negotiate well or push for it assertively as opposed to aggressively.

The end of August is ideal for configuring and discussing plans and projects, as your plans are likely to succeed in the long term. Once Venus enters its own sign of Libra on 29 August you'll feel drawn to finding more peace and harmony in your life.

When Pluto re-enters Capricorn on 3 September, where it will be until 20 November, you'll gain the chance to re-evaluate how you're going so far and to rethink some of your plans and projects, especially from the point of view of who or what is holding you back. You may wish to restructure fundamental aspects of your life so they provide a sense of stability, including your health and wellness routine.

The Virgo new moon on 3 September will help you configure working plans and set them in motion. Be realistic yet optimistic, practical yet inspired in early and mid-September and avoid exaggerated expectations. Financially, this is a good time to avoid overinvesting.

Mid-September will offer the chance for healing developments. Take the initiative and opt for a lovely fitness or well-being update.

The partial lunar eclipse and supermoon in Pisces on 18 September will be a time to dream big, but be sure to keep your feet on the ground while you reach for the stars.

For Virgos

Your sign's ruler, Mercury, will end its retrograde phase on 28 August and will be in Virgo from 9 to 27 September, which will put your focus on finances, communications and relationships. You'll gain the opportunity to make great progress on all fronts, especially if you have spent a little time in the previous weeks reviewing your circumstances in these areas so you can improve your situation in identifiable ways.

However, you must avoid such pitfalls as overwork and unrealistic expectations, as these both lead to stress and potentially to disappointment. You'll find out mid-September whether you have over- or underestimated your circumstances and will get the chance to put things right.

The entry of Venus into Libra on 29 August will put your focus on your self-esteem, making the following three weeks an excellent time to improve this important aspect of your life.

The new moon in Virgo on 3 September signals a fresh cycle in your life, especially if it's your birthday. Mercury in Virgo from 9 September will help improve communications. The partial lunar eclipse supermoon in Pisces on 18 September will spotlight any areas in a personal or business relationship you are unsure of, providing the opportunity to find out more and improve your circumstances.

MONDAY 19 ●

Full moon in Aquarius; sun conjunct Mercury; Jupiter square Saturn; Venus opposite Saturn: a tough day for decisions, especially financial ones. Ensure you have all the details before committing to choices. Moon enters Pisces.

TUESDAY 20 ●

Moon in Pisces.

WEDNESDAY 21 ●

Moon in Pisces.

THURSDAY 22 ●

Sun enters Virgo; sun quincunx Neptune; sun quincunx Pluto: it is time to alter schedules and health routines you've outgrown. Moon in Aries.

FRIDAY 23

Mercury semi-sextile Venus; Mercury trine Chiron; Venus square Mars: a nice day for meetings and romance, but you must avoid sensitive topics; diplomacy will be necessary. Avoid arguments, as they'll ignite quickly. A health or beauty treat will be soothing. Moon in Aries.

SATURDAY 24

Mercury sextile Mars; Venus quincunx Chiron: you'll enjoy a reunion or return to an old haunt. It's a good day to consider how you could help someone, and if you need help it will be available. A health or beauty treat may appeal. Moon in Taurus.

SUNDAY 25

Moon in Taurus.

AUGUST

S	M	T	W	T	F	S
				1	2	3
4	5	6	7	8	9	10
11	12	13	14	15	16	17
18	19	20	21	22	23	24
25	26	27	28	29	30	31

MONDAY 26 ◖

Moon in Gemini.

TUESDAY 27 ◖

Venus trine Uranus: a lovely day to do something different. You may experience a surprise or will feel like being more spontaneous. Moon in Gemini.

WEDNESDAY 28 ◖

Mercury ends its retrograde phase; Venus opposite Neptune: a good day for romance and enjoying the arts and being creative. However, you may feel forgetful, so keep an eye on details. Moon enters Cancer.

THURSDAY 29 ◖

Venus enters Libra; Venus trine Pluto: you'll enjoy getting together with like-minded people. Plans discussed now could be successful in the long term. Moon in Cancer.

FRIDAY 30   (

Moon enters Leo.

SATURDAY 31   (

Mars semi-sextile Uranus: you'll enjoy changing your usual weekend routine.
You may be surprised by someone's news. Moon in Leo.

SUNDAY 1   (

Moon in Leo.

SEPTEMBER

S	M	T	W	T	F	S
1	2	3	4	5	6	7
8	9	10	11	12	13	14
15	16	17	18	19	20	21
22	23	24	25	26	27	28
29	30					

MONDAY 2   (

Mercury trine Chiron: this is a good day for a health appointment. Moon in Virgo.

TUESDAY 3   ○

New moon in Virgo; Pluto enters Capricorn: this is an excellent time to organise and schedule your plans so you're ready to take action when necessary. The next four months will be ideal for reconsidering your options to create more stability in your life.

WEDNESDAY 4   )

Mars enters Cancer; Venus conjunct moon's south node: you'll enjoy a lovely reunion or hearing from someone special. The next few weeks will be ideal for getting in touch with your feelings and for spiritual development. Moon enters Libra.

THURSDAY 5   )

Moon in Libra.

FRIDAY 6   )

Moon in Libra.

SATURDAY 7   )

Moon in Scorpio.

SUNDAY 8   )

*Sun opposite Saturn; Mercury quincunx Neptune: a good time for making
a commitment to someone or something. Just avoid exaggerated expectations
and be real. Moon in Scorpio.*

SEPTEMBER						
S	M	T	W	T	F	S
1	2	3	4	5	6	7
8	9	10	11	12	13	14
15	16	17	18	19	20	21
22	23	24	25	26	27	28
29	30					

MONDAY 9   ☽

Mercury enters Virgo; Mercury quincunx Pluto: the upcoming three weeks will be ideal for focusing on health and work. Focus on details, but avoid obsessing over them. Moon enters Sagittarius.

TUESDAY 10   ☽

Moon in Sagittarius.

WEDNESDAY 11   ☽

Venus quincunx Saturn: a little extra effort will pay off should an obstacle arise. Avoid overspending and expecting things to work out by themselves. Moon in Sagittarius.

THURSDAY 12   ☽

Sun square Jupiter; Mercury sextile Mars: a good day to be practical and avoid exaggerated expectations. Be positive and take the initiative with talks and meetings, but also be realistic. Moon in Capricorn.

FRIDAY 13 ●

Moon in Capricorn.

SATURDAY 14 ●

Sun quincunx Chiron: you'll enjoy resting and perhaps even treating yourself to a healthy indulgence. Avoid minor bumps and scrapes. Moon in Aquarius.

SUNDAY 15 ●

Venus trine Jupiter: you'll enjoy retail therapy and the company of someone special. Just avoid overspending and overindulging as you'll regret it! Moon in Aquarius.

SEPTEMBER

S	M	T	W	T	F	S
1	2	3	4	5	6	7
8	9	10	11	12	13	14
15	16	17	18	19	20	21
22	23	24	25	26	27	28
29	30					

MONDAY 16 ●

Mars square moon's nodes; Venus opposite Chiron: a lovely day for a health or beauty treat. Avoid taking other people's random comments personally. You may be asked for help, and if you need help it will be available. Avoid going against your own principles. Moon in Pisces.

TUESDAY 17 ●

Moon in Pisces.

WEDNESDAY 18 ●

Partial lunar eclipse and supermoon in Pisces; Mercury opposite Saturn: this may be an intense full moon. Be inspired, but be careful with conversations and financial decisions. Some delays may be expected. Moon enters Aries.

THURSDAY 19 ●

Sun trine Uranus: you may experience a welcome surprise or unexpected development. Moon in Aries.

FRIDAY 20 ●

Venus quincunx Uranus: be prepared to stand your ground if necessary, as you may be surprised by developments. Look for common ground to avoid conflict. Moon in Taurus.

SATURDAY 21 ●

Sun opposite Neptune; Mercury square Jupiter; Venus quincunx Neptune: this is a time to be super careful with decisions, as you may be easily influenced. Avoid overspending. This is a romantic time, but you must avoid misunderstandings. Moon in Taurus.

SUNDAY 22 ●

Sun enters Libra; sun trine Pluto; Mercury quincunx Chiron; Venus square Pluto: this is the autumn equinox, a time to integrate ideas, give thanks and prepare for winter. Avoid intense interactions, as they're likely to escalate. It's a good day to rest and avoid minor bumps and scrapes. Romance could blossom but may also be intense. Moon enters Gemini.

SEPTEMBER

S	M	T	W	T	F	S
1	2	3	4	5	6	7
8	9	10	11	12	13	14
15	16	17	18	19	20	21
22	23	24	25	26	27	28
29	30					

september to october 2024

Sun enters Libra, 22 September

As the sun enters Libra it is the autumn equinox, and as the seasons change it's a good time to seek more harmony and balance in your home life as you may be spending more time indoors. Look for balance and a fair go over the coming weeks.

The grand trine at the end of September involving Uranus, Pluto, Mercury, the sun and the moon's south node will be ideal for making bold decisions moving forward. Just ensure you have all the information you need and avoid being easily influenced by unscrupulous yet charming or magnetic people.

Early October will be an excellent time to bring more harmony into your life, so if you feel you need more balance in particular areas this is a good time to put new plans in motion, especially just after the annular solar eclipse on 2 October.

Mid-October will be intense and may involve a surprise. Depending on your sun sign, this will involve love and money or health and well-being. Be prepared to make a bold or even tough call.

The full moon supermoon will be in fiery Aries on 17 October and will spotlight where in life you need to find more balance, especially in the areas of health, nurturance and family. It coincides with the entry of

Venus in the sign of Sagittarius, where it will stay for more than three weeks, encouraging an adventurous, optimistic and proactive approach to life.

For Librans

As the sun enters your sign the big-picture outlook is one of change, making this an excellent time to consider and plan ahead for the transformation you'd like to see in your life. On one hand some projects and ideas will go well, while on the other the tough angle between Venus and Pluto spells tension, especially regarding key relationships and, for some Librans, money.

Key news and developments at the end of September could set you on a fresh course, so be prepared to be flexible and optimistic. When Mercury enters Libra on 26 September it makes a strong link with Pluto, suggesting key talks could move you forward in your projects or personal life. You'll enjoy socialising and networking, and this is a positive time to step into different territory either at work or in a personal relationship.

Despite a potentially intense period in mid-October it's a good time to put yourself on a fresh course health-wise, so make plans to incorporate a new fitness routine or diet if appropriate.

If you find life slightly challenging now, rest assured you'll feel more positive after 17 October. The entry of Venus into the upbeat sign of Sagittarius will coincide with the Aries supermoon, ramping up optimism, but you must avoid conflict if differences of opinion have been prevalent.

MONDAY 23

Venus enters Scorpio: love, money and self-esteem will become focuses, enabling you to steer onto a more favourable path if you feel you've gone astray. Moon in Gemini.

TUESDAY 24

Mercury trine Uranus: you'll enjoy being spontaneous. You may receive unexpected news or travel somewhere different. Moon enters Cancer.

WEDNESDAY 25

Mercury opposite Neptune: be careful with sensitive topics and information and avoid misunderstandings. Romance will appeal, but you may be easily influenced. Moon in Cancer.

THURSDAY 26

Mercury enters Libra; Mercury trine Pluto: a talk or meeting could be transformative. If you'd like to make changes in your life this is the time to instigate them, especially if these involve restructuring and creating a strong foundation. Moon enters Leo.

FRIDAY 27   (

Moon in Leo.

SATURDAY 28   (

Moon in Leo.

SUNDAY 29   (

Sun conjunct moon's south node; sun conjunct Mercury: you'll enjoy a reunion or key news. A trip may appeal. Moon enters Virgo.

SEPTEMBER

S	M	T	W	T	F	S
1	2	3	4	5	6	7
8	9	10	11	12	13	14
15	16	17	18	19	20	21
22	23	24	25	26	27	28
29	30					

MONDAY 30   (

Mercury conjunct moon's south node; Mars trine Saturn: another lovely day for a reunion. You may receive key news or undertake an important trip. It's a good time to take the initiative with carefully laid plans. Moon in Virgo.

TUESDAY 1   (

Moon in Virgo.

WEDNESDAY 2   ○

Solar eclipse in Libra: a good time to place your intention on gaining more balance and peace in your life. A place or person from your past may be a part of your decision-making.

THURSDAY 3   )

Mercury semi-sextile Venus: a good day for get-togethers and for financial decision-making. Moon in Libra.

FRIDAY 4   )

*Venus trine Saturn: a lovely day for get-togethers, both at work and socially.
A financial matter may be decided upon. If you are shopping, avoid
overspending as you may regret it! Moon enters Scorpio.*

SATURDAY 5   )

Moon in Scorpio.

SUNDAY 6   )

*Mercury square Mars: avoid rash decision-making and be prepared for
complex communications or even traffic delays by planning ahead.
Moon in Scorpio.*

OCTOBER						
S	M	T	W	T	F	S
		1	2	3	4	5
6	7	8	9	10	11	12
13	14	15	16	17	18	19
20	21	22	23	24	25	26
27	28	29	30	31		

MONDAY 7 ☽

Moon in Sagittarius.

TUESDAY 8 ☽

Mercury opposite Chiron; Mercury trine Jupiter; Venus trine Mars: a good day for a health appointment, travel, progressing projects, meetings and financial decisions. If you're shopping, avoid overspending as you're likely to regret it. Romance could also flourish. Moon in Sagittarius.

WEDNESDAY 9 ☽

Moon enters Capricorn.

THURSDAY 10 ☽

Moon in Capricorn.

FRIDAY 11

Mercury quincunx Uranus: be prepared to go the extra mile to gain the results you want; you won't regret it. Moon enters Aquarius.

SATURDAY 12

Mercury quincunx Neptune: some conversations or travel may be complex or delayed but your efforts will be worthwhile. Moon in Aquarius.

SUNDAY 13

Mercury enters Scorpio; Mercury square Pluto: some conversations and projects may be more intense than you'd prefer, so be sure to plan ahead to avoid unnecessary disappointment. Moon enters Pisces.

OCTOBER

S	M	T	W	T	F	S
		1	2	3	4	5
6	7	8	9	10	11	12
13	14	15	16	17	18	19
20	21	22	23	24	25	26
27	28	29	30	31		

MONDAY 14   ●

Sun opposite Chiron; sun and Chiron square Mars; Venus opposite Uranus: this is a good day to consider health and well-being above all else. Avoid rash decision-making and feeling under pressure; take time out when you can. Moon in Pisces.

TUESDAY 15   ●

Moon enters Aries.

WEDNESDAY 16   ●

Venus trine Neptune: romance, the arts and spirituality will flourish under these skies. Moon in Aries.

THURSDAY 17   ●

Full moon supermoon in Aries; Venus enters Sagittarius: this full moon will shine a light on where you need to find more balance, especially in the areas of health, nurturance and family. Moon enters Taurus.

FRIDAY 18 ●

Moon in Taurus.

SATURDAY 19 ●

Sun quincunx Uranus: unusual or unexpected circumstances needn't put you off track. Rise to the challenge and you'll enjoy your day. Moon enters Gemini.

SUNDAY 20 ●

Sun quincunx Neptune: you'll enjoy romance and the arts, but you must avoid overindulgence and overspending as you're likely to regret it! Moon in Gemini.

OCTOBER

S	M	T	W	T	F	S
		1	2	3	4	5
6	7	8	9	10	11	12
13	14	15	16	17	18	19
20	21	22	23	24	25	26
27	28	29	30	31		

october to november 2024

Sun enters Scorpio, 22 October

As the sun enters passionate Scorpio it aspects intense Pluto, the ruler of Scorpio. You may manage to avoid drama and navigate into calm seas, but you must avoid conflict. On a lighter note, if you work towards your goals you will succeed.

The end of October is an ideal time to be realistic and avoid stirring a hornet's nest. Tread carefully and see obstacles as opportunities that will bring about a healing and healthier path forward. The beginning of November is especially conducive to healing and spiritual and health-related progress.

Mars in Leo from 4 November will bring a more adventurous and energetic frame of mind but you must avoid a gung-ho or impulsive approach, which can backfire. Luckily, once Venus has entered earthy Capricorn on 11 November you'll find it much easier to ground your plans and make progress in small, constructive steps.

Nevertheless, you're best to match delicate negotiations and communications with careful research to avoid mistakes during November.

When Pluto enters Aquarius on 20 November expect a change of focus. You're ready for something new, so avoid feeling tied to the past because it's time to embrace a well thought-out plan. If you haven't devised a plan for something different and exciting in your life, there's no time like the present!

For Scorpios

While this is potentially a transformative and empowering time, you risk conflict and arguments unless you're careful with intense circumstances at the end of October. The Mercury–Uranus opposition on 30 October will bring unexpected developments you're best to navigate with the full facts at your fingertips, as you may otherwise be prone to making decisions based on assumptions rather than information.

The new moon in your sign on 1 November will present opportunities to boost your circumstances; however, the opposition between Mars and Pluto, your sign's rulers, can spell an intense time. If you channel your energy into productive projects you could move mountains, but if you succumb to petty arguments and conflict this is likely to be an explosive time.

As Mars enters Leo on 4 November you could turn a corner within any contentious or stressful areas, but you must be careful to avoid making rash decisions. Focus on keeping expectations realistic around 11 November and again you could move mountains. You may also discover at this time whether your plans need a little more work in order to succeed.

On 20 November your sign's traditional ruler, Pluto, will re-enter Aquarius, the sign associated with ingenuity and excitement. It's time to embrace these qualities in your life, and the readier you are to do so the more you'll appreciate this considerable change of focus in your life. For many this will involve travel, finances and communications, and for some a key relationship.

MONDAY 21

Moon enters Cancer.

TUESDAY 22

Sun enters Scorpio; sun square Pluto: welcome to a passionate, upbeat and potentially intense four weeks. Today especially may bring certain contentious issues into focus, so it is best to tread carefully to avoid conflict. Moon in Cancer.

WEDNESDAY 23

Venus trine moon's north node: you'll enjoy getting together with or hearing from someone you admire. Moon in Cancer.

THURSDAY 24

Moon in Leo.

FRIDAY 25 ◐

Mars sextile Uranus: you'll appreciate a change of routine or a surprise. Be spontaneous. Moon in Leo.

SATURDAY 26 ◐

Moon enters Virgo.

SUNDAY 27 ◐

Mercury quincunx Chiron: a good day for a rest, a healthy activity and sports and to relax. Moon in Virgo.

OCTOBER

S	M	T	W	T	F	S
		1	2	3	4	5
6	7	8	9	10	11	12
13	14	15	16	17	18	19
20	21	22	23	24	25	26
27	28	29	30	31		

MONDAY 28   (

Sun sesquiquadrate Jupiter; Venus square Saturn; Mars trine Neptune: a lovely day for romance, but you must avoid pre-empting an outcome. Keep an eye on personal, work and financial matters and avoid making rash decisions and having overly high expectations. Moon in Virgo.

TUESDAY 29   (

Moon in Libra.

WEDNESDAY 30   (

Mercury opposite Uranus: unusual or unexpected news and developments are on the way. Be creative and avoid making rash decisions. Moon in Libra.

THURSDAY 31   (

Moon enters Scorpio.

FRIDAY 1 ○

New moon in Scorpio; Mercury trine Neptune and Mars: this is a powerful new moon, especially if it's your birthday. Make a wish but be careful what you wish for, as it's likely to come true!

SATURDAY 2 ☽

Jupiter sextile Chiron: a good day for mending bridges with someone you have quarrelled with and for boosting health, relationships and wealth. Moon in Scorpio.

SUNDAY 3 ☽

Venus trine Chiron; Venus opposite Jupiter; Mars opposition Pluto: this could be a healing and creative time, but risks being fraught with tension and conflict. Moon in Sagittarius.

NOVEMBER

S	M	T	W	T	F	S
					1	2
3	4	5	6	7	8	9
10	11	12	13	14	15	16
17	18	19	20	21	22	23
24	25	26	27	28	29	30

MONDAY 4)

Mars enters Leo; sun trine Saturn: a good day to put in place carefully laid plans. A commitment or agreement can be made. You're likely to feel more adventurous about your plans over the coming weeks. Moon in Sagittarius.

TUESDAY 5)

Moon enters Capricorn.

WEDNESDAY 6)

Moon in Capricorn.

THURSDAY 7)

Mercury trine moon's north node: a lovely day for get-togethers. Moon enters Aquarius.

FRIDAY 8 ☽

Venus quincunx Uranus: you'll welcome a change of routine, even if it's a little stressful. If obstacles arise you'll overcome them with a positive, diligent approach. Moon in Aquarius.

SATURDAY 9 ☽

Venus square Neptune: you'll appreciate the opportunity to relax but may also be prone to making mistakes and misplacing valuables. Avoid overspending and overindulging as you'll regret it! Moon in Aquarius.

SUNDAY 10 ☽

Moon in Pisces.

NOVEMBER

S	M	T	W	T	F	S
					1	2
3	4	5	6	7	8	9
10	11	12	13	14	15	16
17	18	19	20	21	22	23
24	25	26	27	28	29	30

MONDAY 11 ●

Venus enters Capricorn; sun quincunx Jupiter and Chiron: a little Mondayitis may arise and a tense or difficult circumstance is best taken in small steps to avoid feeling overwhelmed. Look after your health and well-being before anything else. Moon in Pisces.

TUESDAY 12 ●

Mercury square Saturn: engage in communications and make financial decisions carefully to avoid tension, mistakes, delays and mix-ups. When you do you could progress and make valuable commitments. Moon in Aries.

WEDNESDAY 13 ●

Moon in Aries.

THURSDAY 14 ●

Moon in Taurus.

FRIDAY 15 ●

Full moon in Taurus: this full moon will spotlight where in your life you may need to be a little more spontaneous, as a surprise emerges.

SATURDAY 16 ●

Sun opposite Uranus; Venus square moon's nodes: be prepared for something unexpected to occur, unless you already recently experienced a surprise. A change of environment or of circumstance will appeal. A difference of opinion is likely to arise or an obstacle, so be adaptable for the best results. Moon in Gemini.

SUNDAY 17 ●

Moon in Gemini.

NOVEMBER

S	M	T	W	T	F	S
					1	2
3	4	5	6	7	8	9
10	11	12	13	14	15	16
17	18	19	20	21	22	23
24	25	26	27	28	29	30

MONDAY 18 ●

Mercury opposite Jupiter: your ideas may not coincide with someone else's but you can establish common ground. A trip, news or meeting will be significant. Moon in Cancer.

TUESDAY 19 ●

Sun trine Neptune; Mercury trine Chiron: a good day for a beauty or health treat and a trip somewhere beautiful. Romance could thrive, but you must avoid making assumptions. Moon in Cancer.

WEDNESDAY 20 ●

Pluto enters Aquarius; Venus sesquiquadrate Uranus: it's time to embrace something original and exciting in your life. Be prepared to make changes! Moon enters Leo.

THURSDAY 21 ●

Sun enters Sagittarius; sun sextile Pluto: a lovely time to embrace a fresh outlook in your life. Be prepared to make original and long-term changes. Moon in Leo.

FRIDAY 22 ◖

Venus sextile Saturn: a good day for making a commitment in your personal life and financially and at work. Romance could blossom. Moon enters Virgo.

SATURDAY 23 ◖

Mars trine moon's north node: a lovely day for get-togethers. You may meet someone you feel is familiar, even if you have never met before. Moon in Virgo.

SUNDAY 24 ◖

Moon in Virgo.

NOVEMBER						
S	M	T	W	T	F	S
					1	2
3	4	5	6	7	8	9
10	11	12	13	14	15	16
17	18	19	20	21	22	23
24	25	26	27	28	29	30

November to December 2024

Sun enters Sagittarius, 21 November

Just as the sun enters Sagittarius it makes a harmonious angle (sextile/60 degrees) with transformative Pluto, suggesting this is an excellent time to go ahead and make long-term and deep changes in your life as your efforts are likely to succeed.

The period 21 to 26 November has lovely aspects that will support romance and making firm commitments to your various projects and collaborators, both in your personal life and at work.

Mercury turns retrograde on 26 November, making the days beforehand ideal for tying up loose ends in paperwork and agreements. A trip or news at this time may be significant. You will gain the chance to review and reassess your plans over the ensuing few weeks if you feel you have not completed your projects up to this date as well as you'd hoped.

The new moon in Sagittarius on 1 December is an ideal time to be adventurous in your life and consider how you might make progress with your more outgoing plans, such as those concerning travel, study and spiritual endeavours. Build strong foundations around your projects and they will succeed in the long term.

Mars also turns retrograde on 6 December, which could lead to a lack of energy. To avoid feeling depleted, consider following a healthy, energy-boosting diet and fitness plan for the rest of December.

For Sagittarians

Mercury will turn retrograde in your sign on 26 November, providing you with a few days beforehand to tie up loose ends with paperwork and projects to avoid unnecessary delays over the ensuing weeks. If you're unable to do so rest assured you will get the time later, and the opportunity to review matters over the coming weeks may work in your favour.

You may be drawn to revisiting an old haunt or reconnecting with friends or even an old flame. Some or all of these eventualities will provide a healing experience, enabling you to move ahead.

The new moon in your sign on 1 December is ideal for building stability and security, especially in your personal life for November-born Sagittarians and work-wise and in your daily and health routine for December-born Archers.

Be prepared to enter new territory early in December, as the Venus–Pluto conjunction will ask that you view someone or something in your life from a fresh perspective. You may need to rethink old habits or even return to an old haunt to do so.

The period 19 to 20 December will be particularly positive for making progress with your carefully laid plans, but you must be super careful with both emotional and financial investments at this time.

MONDAY 25   ☽

Moon enters Libra.

TUESDAY 26   ☽

Mercury turns retrograde; sun trine moon's north node; Venus quincunx Jupiter: a lovely time for meetings and get-togethers. Just ensure you keep expectations realistic and get paperwork tied up by today to avoid future delays. Moon in Libra.

WEDNESDAY 27   ☽

Sun trine Mars: your projects and activities are likely to progress under their own steam, so ensure you're happy with the direction they're going in. Moon in Libra.

THURSDAY 28   ☽

Venus square Chiron: avoid delays by planning ahead. Also avoid taking other people's random comments personally, unless criticism is merited. You may offer someone help, and if you need advice it is available. Moon in Scorpio.

FRIDAY 29 ☾

Mercury semi-sextile Venus: a lovely opportunity to catch up with someone special and to set a past matter straight, especially in connection with money, love and romance. Moon in Scorpio.

SATURDAY 30 ☾

Moon enters Sagittarius.

SUNDAY 1 ○

New moon in Sagittarius: a good time to make a wish and be adventurous. Your long-term plans will succeed if you lay solid foundations for them.

DECEMBER

S	M	T	W	T	F	S
1	2	3	4	5	6	7
8	9	10	11	12	13	14
15	16	17	18	19	20	21
22	23	24	25	26	27	28
29	30	31				

MONDAY 2)

Mercury trine Chiron; Venus trine Uranus: a good day to review health and well-being and for a reunion or return to an old haunt. A pleasant surprise will be appreciated. Moon enters Capricorn.

TUESDAY 3)

Moon in Capricorn.

WEDNESDAY 4)

Sun square Saturn; Mercury opposite Jupiter; Venus sextile Neptune: what is holding you back? If it's you, find ways to banish anxiety or fear. If it's someone else consider building bridges or, ultimately, choosing a different path. Be inspired. Moon in Capricorn.

THURSDAY 5)

Moon in Aquarius.

FRIDAY 6 ❯

Mars turns retrograde; sun conjunct Mercury: a reunion or return to a familiar place will be key to moving forward, even if you must first overcome an obstacle. Moon in Aquarius.

SATURDAY 7 ❯

Venus enters Aquarius; sun opposite Jupiter; Venus conjunct Pluto: a good day for a get-together and to discuss important matters. A trip or visit will be key, but you must avoid arguments. An intense day. Romance could flourish. Moon in Pisces.

SUNDAY 8 ❯

Moon in Pisces.

DECEMBER

S	M	T	W	T	F	S
1	2	3	4	5	6	7
8	9	10	11	12	13	14
15	16	17	18	19	20	21
22	23	24	25	26	27	28
29	30	31				

MONDAY 9 ◗

Moon enters Aries.

TUESDAY 10 ◗

Sun trine Chiron; Venus sextile moon's north node: a healing day in which common ground can be sought with someone important. A health or beauty treat may appeal. Moon in Aries.

WEDNESDAY 11 ◗

Moon enters Taurus.

THURSDAY 12 ●

Venus opposite Mars: a difference of opinion needn't mean you must cross swords. Romance could flourish, but be sure to avoid contentious topics if possible. Moon in Taurus.

FRIDAY 13 ●

Mercury sextile Venus: despite it being Friday the 13th it's a good day for a reunion and for work and financial talks. Romance could flourish. Moon enters Gemini.

SATURDAY 14 ●

Moon in Gemini.

SUNDAY 15 ●

Full moon in Gemini; sun quincunx Uranus; Mercury ends its retrograde phase: this full moon will shine a light on travel, your projects and wishes for those close to you and your relationships. An unexpected or unusual development will merit focus. Moon enters Cancer.

DECEMBER

S	M	T	W	T	F	S
1	2	3	4	5	6	7
8	9	10	11	12	13	14
15	16	17	18	19	20	21
22	23	24	25	26	27	28
29	30	31				

MONDAY 16   ●

Moon in Cancer.

TUESDAY 17   ●

Moon enters Leo.

WEDNESDAY 18   ●

Sun square Neptune: be careful with details at work to avoid misunderstandings and mix-ups. Avoid being forgetful and daydreaming. Moon in Leo.

THURSDAY 19   ●

Venus semi-sextile Saturn: finances, negotiations, travel and romance could thrive but you must avoid making assumptions. Moon in Leo.

FRIDAY 20

Venus trine Jupiter: a good day to be optimistic and outgoing and embrace a progressive mindset. Moon enters Virgo.

SATURDAY 21

Sun enters Capricorn: this is the winter solstice. The next four weeks will be ideal for taking things one step at a time. Pace yourself! Moon in Virgo.

SUNDAY 22

Sun semi-sextile Pluto: this is a good time to lay the framework for any changes you feel are necessary. Moon enters Libra.

DECEMBER

S	M	T	W	T	F	S
1	2	3	4	5	6	7
8	9	10	11	12	13	14
15	16	17	18	19	20	21
22	23	24	25	26	27	28
29	30	31				

December 2024

Sun enters Capricorn, 21 December

As the sun steps into Capricorn it is the winter solstice, a time to assess the year that has been, bring healing to those areas you feel could have gone better, celebrate your successes and prepare for the new year of 2025.

Christmas is often a tense time of year, even though peace and rest are always hoped for. This year an additional strain due to delays in travel, misunderstandings and communication mix-ups could add stress to an already tense time, so additional care and attention towards creating a healing atmosphere may be necessary.

The new year will include a focus on well-being, health and healing. You may be drawn to enjoying a different type of New Year's Eve celebration than usual, one that brings peace and harmony into your New Year's Day.

For more about Capricorn in January 2025 reserve your copy of the 2025 Astrology Diary. See Rockpool Publishing at www.rockpoolpublishing.com.au and www.patsybennett.com.

Wishing everyone a very happy solstice, Yuletide and New Year!

For Capricorns

You prefer life to progress one step at a time and prefer to avoid feeling overwhelmed whenever possible. This December it will be in your interest to find ways to earth your plans and projects to avoid disappointment, as choppy skies will otherwise interrupt your usual and preferred way of doing things.

The new moon in your sign on 30 December is an especially potent time to focus on the way you'd prefer 2025 to roll out. As always, though, be careful what you wish for as it will surely come true. In other words, do your research carefully and plan ahead for rosy skies.

MONDAY 23 ◖

Sun square moon's nodes: you may not agree with everyone or be happy with some of your projects, but if you look for balance and take things methodically and calmly you will succeed. Moon in Libra.

TUESDAY 24 ◖

Venus sextile Chiron; Saturn square Jupiter: will you focus on the positives or the negatives? Take a moment to reappraise circumstances and be optimistic. A healing message or meeting will arise. Moon in Libra.

WEDNESDAY 25 ◖

Sun quincunx Mars: a hastily spoken word needn't break an otherwise peaceful day. Focus on the positives. Moon enters Scorpio.

THURSDAY 26 ◖

Mercury opposite Jupiter: travel, communications and meetings may be delayed or present obstacles, so ensure you plan ahead to avoid frustrations. Moon in Scorpio.

FRIDAY 27   (

Mercury square Saturn: be prepared to plan ahead with travel and avoid contentious topics in communications. Misunderstandings are likely, so be patient. Moon enters Sagittarius.

SATURDAY 28   (

Venus square Uranus: expect an unusual or unanticipated development. Avoid impulsiveness and take time to consider your options. Moon in Sagittarius.

SUNDAY 29   (

Moon in Sagittarius.

DECEMBER

S	M	T	W	T	F	S
1	2	3	4	5	6	7
8	9	10	11	12	13	14
15	16	17	18	19	20	21
22	23	24	25	26	27	28
29	30	31				

MONDAY 30 ○

New moon in Capricorn: this is a good time to consider your options carefully and again avoid impulsiveness.

TUESDAY 31)

Mercury trine Chiron: there is a focus on health and healing this New Year's Eve. It's a great time to bring a sense of serenity to your life, as the stars will help you. Someone special may need your help, and if you need advice or guidance it will be available. Moon in Capricorn.

WEDNESDAY 1)

THURSDAY 2)

NOTES

NOTES

NOTES

About the author

Patsy Bennett is a rare combination of astrologer and psychic medium. Her horoscopes are published in newspapers and magazines in Australia and internationally and she has written freelance for publications including *Nature and Health* and *Practical Parenting*. Patsy has appeared on several live daytime TV and radio shows, including *Studio 10* and *The Project*. Her books *Sun Sign Secrets*, *Astrology: Secrets of the moon*, *2024 Horoscopes*, the yearly astrology diaries and *Zodiac Moon Reading Cards* are published by Rockpool Publishing.

Born in New Zealand, Patsy relocated to the UK where, in the 1980s, she worked as a sub-editor and production editor for women's and fashion magazines including *Woman's Own* and *ELLE*. She studied astrology at the Faculty of Astrological Studies in London in the 1990s and in 1998 relocated to Australia, where she worked as a reporter for local newspapers in the northern New South Wales area, wrote freelance for magazines and continued her practice as an astrologer.

Patsy has worked as a professional astrologer and medium for more than 25 years. She began reading palms and tarot at the age of 14, and experienced mediumistic insights as young as 12. She is a natural medium and has perfected her skill by studying with some of the world's foremost and experienced mediums. She provides astrology and psychic intuitive consultations and facilitates astrology and psychic development workshops in northern New South Wales and on the Gold Coast.

Patsy gained a Master of Arts degree in Romance Languages and Literature at the University of London and taught at the University of California, Berkeley. She is a member of the Queensland Federation of Astrologers and the Spiritualists' National Union.

She runs www.astrocast.com.au, www.patsybennett.com, facebook @patsybennettpsychicastrology and instagram @patsybennettastrology.

further reading of astronomical data

The American Ephemeris for the 21st Century 2000 to 2050, Michelsen, ACS Publications.
Computer programs of astronomical data: Solar Fire, Esoteric Technologies Pty Ltd.

Also by patsy Bennett

Sun Sign Secrets
Celestial guidance with the sun, moon and stars

ISBN: 9781925946352

This comprehensive, ground-breaking astrology book is for everyone who wants to make the most of their true potential and be in the flow with solar and lunar phases. It includes analyses of each sun sign from Aries to Pisces and pinpoints how you can dynamically make the most of your life in real time alongside celestial events. Work with the gifts and strengths of your sun sign in relation to every lunar phase, zodiacal month, new moon, full moon and eclipse.

Look up your sun sign to read all about your talents and potential pitfalls, and discover how to express your inner star power during the various phases of the sun and moon throughout the days, months and years to come.

Available at all good bookstores.

2024 Horoscopes

365 daily predictions for every zodiac sign

ISBN: 9781922785190

This is the only horoscope book you'll need in 2024! This complete astrological guide contains inspiring and motivational forecasts for 2024 so you can be well prepared for the year ahead. You will discover how to best navigate your opportunities and reach your full potential.

2024 Horoscopes features daily horoscope predictions for all signs that explain what you can expect and the ideal days to attract wealth, love, success and more. This book also includes a yearly overview of your love life, money, home life, career and health.

Available at all good bookstores.